D0199627

21928

A Biblical Approach to Personal Suffering

by
Walter C. Kaiser, Jr.

MOODY PRESS
CHICAGO

Library
Oakland S.U.M.

Copyright © 1982 by
THE MOODY BIBLE INSTITUTE
OF CHICAGO

All rights reserved. No part of this book may be reproduced
in any form without permission in writing from the publisher,
except in the case of brief quotations embodied in critical
articles or reviews.

The use of selected references from various versions of the
Bible in this publication does not necessarily imply publisher
endorsement of the version in its entirety.

Material from *Five Smooth Stones for Pastoral Work* by
Eugene Peterson, © 1980 by John Knox Press, is used by
permission.

Library of Congress Cataloging in Publication Data

Kaiser, Walter C.
  A Biblical approach to personal suffering.
  Includes bibliographical references.
  1. Bible. O.T. Lamentations—Criticism, interpretation, etc.
2. Suffering—Biblical teaching. I Title.

BS1535.2.K34   224'.307   82-2232

ISBN 0-8024-4634-5   AACR2

1 2 3 4 5 6 7 Printing/LC/Year 87 86 85 84 83 82
Printed in the United States of America

To the Reverend Carroll A. Nelson—Pastor, seminary placement director, seminary chaplain, colleague, and special friend who has had heavy physical pain as a constant companion for many years while cheerfully testifying that God's grace is indeed sufficient. Carroll has shown us what doxological suffering is.

And to the memory of the Reverend Arne B. Hansen (May 16, 1922—August 19, 1981)—A special friend, faculty colleague, and pastor of pastors whose own bout with suffering at the conclusion of his earthly life taught all of us at Trinity Evangelical Divinity School how to face suffering confident of our Lord's faithfulness when the familiar supports of life seemed to crumble. Arne was a living example of evidential or testimonial suffering.

"Great is Thy faithfulness"—Lamentations 3:23

Contents

Preface

One of life's most puzzling problems has been the enigma of the presence, persistence, and power of the evil, pain, and suffering experienced by mortals. "Why," we all seem to ask, "is this happening to me? Why is all of this necessary? Will there never be an end to the mental distress which comes from suffering?"

The difficulty is only sharpened all the more for the believer who attempts to explain how a good God can permit hardship and suffering that weigh so heavily on even the most faithful of His children. What can be done to avoid suffering, if anything? What is one to do when he or she is in the midst of such anguish? Can anything be said to comfort and aid a friend or loved one who is deep in the throes of suffering?

The Old Testament contains one of the most comprehensive surveys of the problem of suffering found anywhere. However, the emphasis of those writers fell on the purpose and result of suffering rather than on the definition, origin, or even rationale for suffering. They were fully persuaded that ours is a moral order guided by a merciful, benevolent, and gracious Lord who is actively involved with the current plight and daily affairs of all men, nations, and events. Although believing men and women might have grown impatient and perplexed over what appeared to them to be disparities and inequities between the prosperity of the wicked and the grief of the righteous, still the Old Testament was firmly convinced that God's moral order in the governing of the universe would be vindicated.

In the book of Lamentations, more than perhaps anywhere else except for its individualistic expression in the book of

Job, we are led into an experience of suffering and communal pain on a scale seldom endured by many individuals or nations. All too frequently the subject of suffering is avoided, or the realities of human pathos and divine involvement are minimized. Lamentations will not yield to any of these cheap "cures." Instead of panaceas, it will direct us to the faithfulness and gracious character of our God.

No book of the Bible is more of an orphan book than Lamentations; rarely, if ever, have interpreters chosen to use this book for a Bible study, an expository series of messages, or as a Bible conference textual exposition. Our generation's neglect of this volume has meant that our pastoral work, our caring ministry for believers, and our own ability to find direction in the midst of calamity, pain, and suffering have been seriously truncated and rendered partially or totally ineffective.

The apostle Paul was able to say after three years of ministry at Ephesus that he had not failed to declare to the Ephesian church "The whole counsel of God" (Acts 20:27). Surely, he must have taught them how to face suffering. And what better way to teach such realities than by leading God's people in a study of this grossly neglected segment of God's word? Can you as a Bible teacher, daily reader of Scripture, or a pastor charged with the spiritual nurture of your people conclude as Paul did that you have not neglected any area of the biblical canon in your own growth or in the development of those under your care? The point is this: Any time we neglect any portion of the full biblical revelation of God— be it ever so minor in comparison to some of the central affirmations of our faith—we are providing the enemy of our souls with a seedbed for planting heresies or doubts. Let us then make full proof of our ministries and "study to show ourselves approved unto God as workmen not needing to be ashamed" (cf. 2 Tim. 2:15). May this volume prove helpful as we fulfill this obligation together.

I must express my gratitude to our Lord for His help and strength in composing these chapters in the midst of newly assumed administrative duties, class preparations, and a heavy schedule of speaking. The reward has come already in the way that Lamentations has ministered to my own heart with a whole new vision of the One whose faithfulness never fails.

Numerous other friends have faithfully ministered to bring this project to fruition. Those who deserve special mention are: Philip Rawley, Moody Press textbook editor, whose interest in the project kept us going during the slowdowns; my wife Margaret Ruth, my secretary Lois Armstrong, and secretaries Marty Irwin and Sherry Kull, who each typed various sections of the manuscript; and my graduate assistant Timothy Addington, who helped with the proofreading and indexes. I am grateful to our Lord for the significant part each of these choice servants of God played in bringing this manuscript to publication. One final note: Unless otherwise noted, all translations of the biblical text are my own.

Introduction

Lamentations is eminently suited to treat one of the most perplexing and devastating problems of all human existence: suffering and communal pain on the large scale of national grief. It is impossible to overestimate the intensity or the depth of suffering that resulted from the fall of Jerusalem in 587 B.C. The worst that could happen anywhere to any nation, city, house of worship, or person, happened here— earth's loneliest moment of suffering!

> Look, O Lord, and notice
> whom you have treated so.
> Should women eat their offspring,
> the children of their tender care?
> Should priest and prophet be slain
> in the sanctuary of the Lord?
> In the dirt of the streets they lie,
> the young and the old.
> My maidens and my young men
> have fallen by the sword.
> You have slain them in the day of your anger;
> you have slaughtered them without mercy.
> You invited, as on the day of an appointed feast,
> my terrors on every side,
> And on the day of the anger of the Lord
> there were none who escaped or remained;
> My enemy has wiped out
> those whom I cared for and brought up. [Lam. 2:20-22]

Lamentations kept alive in the life of Israel the memory of that tragic event of the fall of Jerusalem. But it also has a

13

function for all the people of God in all times in that it wants us to deal with suffering

> in such a way as to direct the despair which ordinarily accompanies guilt *towards* God and not *away from* him. . . . Suffering, in itself, does not lead a person into a deeper relationship with God. It is just as liable to do the opposite, dehumanizing and embittering [one]. The person who experiences suffering can mistakenly interpret the experience as the rejection of God, concluding that because God hates sin, he also hates the sinner. . . .
>
> The task of pastoral work is to comfort without in any way avoiding the human realities of guilt or denying the divine realities of judgment. There is no better place for learning how to do that than in Lamentations. In the midst of suffering Lamentations keeps attention on the God who loves his people so that the judgment does not become impersonal nor the guilt of the people neurotic, nor the misfortune merely general. It pays attention to the exact ways in which suffering takes place; it takes with absolute seriousness the feelings that follow in the wake of judgment; and then it shapes these sufferings and feelings into forms of response to God. Pain thus becomes accessible to compassion.[1]

Suffering cannot adequately be dealt with by pretending that it does not exist. It will do no good to try to minimize it or to "talk" it out of existence. It *does* exist and it *does* hurt. Nor will it do any good to search for a sudden cure for its pain as if one, by swallowing a miracle pill of modern pharmacology, could remove all at once the heavy weight it imposes.

The most comforting news Scripture has for the sufferer is that where pain, grief, and hurt are, there is God. Instead of a panacea, our Lord offers His presence. One of the greatest promises in the Bible, which speaks to all our fears, is bound up in the very name of our Lord—Immanuel: "God with us."

Along with this assurance of the presence of our Lord

comes perspective into the way pain and suffering can work to bring a better perception of our situation, times, and needs vis-à-vis the upward calling of God in all our lives. This perception, moreover, is increased when we allow our pain and grief to be shared with others—especially with the community of faith. Only a selfish and inverse pride would insist on isolating oneself from sharing personal or national grief with others. Lamentations will teach us how to sharpen our response to this greatest of all human difficulties by working through it in ways that accomplish the purposes of God in our lives.

Of course, there are alternatives to the biblically-sanctioned response, but will they accomplish the purposes of God? Should we have been hurt and suffered so much to emerge with merely a socially acceptable solution? Lamentations would have us emerge with more than the temporal healing; why not learn simultaneously that "the Lord is my portion" (Lam. 3:24)?

The Literary Form

Even the literary style in which this book was cast appears to have a definite purpose. Chapters 1-4 are composed in an alphabetic structure as acrostics.[2] Each of the twenty-two letters of the Hebrew alphabet is represented in its usual order, one letter for each stanza of the poem in chapter 1, but in chapters 2-4 the letters corresponding approximately to *o* and *p* in our English alphabet are transposed.

Normally the acrostic was used to aid in memorizing and retaining the content and sequence of some written or oral material, but that will hardly prove to be the reason here.[3] How could any Jew ever forget the loss and pain suffered in 587 B.C.? Rather, the purpose was to make sure that the grounds of the grief and suffering were worked through completely. No facet should be left out; every detail of the human tragedy must be itemized and expressed completely.

Eugene H. Peterson has captured this truth most poignantly:

> One of the commonest ways to deal with another's suffering is to make light of it, to gloss it over, to attempt shortcuts through it. Because it is so painful, we try to get to the other side quickly. Lamentations provides a structure to guarantee against that happening. A regular Talmudic idiom speaks of keeping the Torah [the first five books of the Old Testament] from *aleph* to *tau* or, as we would say, from A to Z. Lamentations puts the idiom to work by being attentive to suffering. It is important to pay attention to everything that God says; but it is also important to pay attention to everything that men and women feel, especially when that feeling is as full of pain and puzzlement as suffering.
>
> The acrostic is a structure for taking suffering seriously . . . [Lamentations] *repeats* the acrostic form. It goes over the story again and again and again and again and again—five times.[4]

The first three chapters have the same grouping-patterns that involve three lines to a stanza.[5] In chapters 1 and 2, each three-line stanza begins with the next letter of the alphabet. But a *crescendo* (an increase in loudness and intensity) is signaled in chapter 3 when each of the three lines begins with the same letter of the alphabet and is given separate verse numbers. The fourth poem only contains two lines to each stanza and thus indicates a *decrescendo* (a gradual decrease in loudness or intensity). The last chapter is the only poem that is not an acrostic even though it simulates the shape and form of an acrostic in that it has twenty-two verses and resembles certain prayers of corporate lament such as Psalms 44 and 80.

The lament moves to a high pitch of excitement and intensity in chapter 3 and then decreases in strength until the case is laid at God's feet in prayer—but only after the *fullness* of the people's grief has been gone over from *a* to *z*. Likewise, the expression of what would otherwise be boundless grief finds containment and bounds in the device of the acrostic. When the final letter is reached, the lament should have spent itself. There will come a moment when it can be written, "Enough."

Peterson's observations once again prove to be most helpful: " Evil is not inexhaustible. It is not infinite. It is not worthy of a lifetime of attention. Timing is important. If a terminus is proposed too soon, people know that their suffering has not been taken seriously and conclude that it is therefore without significance. But if it goes on too long . . . [it can become] a crippled adjustment to life which frustrates wholeness. 'To some, ill health is a way to be important.' "⁶

Thus the acrostic form contributes to the meaning and significance of all serious discomfort, each hurt, loss, disease, or tragedy. It patiently goes over each step in the process. It systematically organizes each detail so as to identify, objectify, and pacify each and every pain. It also sets boundaries to suffering so that mortals are not left forever numb and mute in the horrid face of jumbled confusion that evil has introduced into their lives. The final letter will come and so will the end of this sorrow. Nothing troubles the sufferer more than the feeling of the endlessness of one's misery. Therefore the acrostic will help to itemize, organize, and finalize grief.

THE HISTORY OF THE JERUSALEM TRAGEDY

The capture of Jerusalem and the tragic burning of the Temple in 587 B.C. by the Babylonians is the sad background for the poems of Lamentations. The only proper name included in the book is that of Edom (4:22), but the historical connections and allusions to events chronicled in 2 Kings 25 and in Jeremiah are unmistakable.⁷ Some of the key points of comparison may be seen by using three parallel columns with the narrative of 2 Kings 25 as a guide. They include:

	2 Kings 25 (See also 2 Chron. 36:11-21)	*Jeremiah*	*Lamentations*
1. The siege of Jeru- salem	1-2	39:1-3; 52:4-5	2:20-22; 3:5, 7
2. The famine in the city	3	37:21; 52:6	1:11, 19; 2:11- 12; 2:19-20; 4:4- 5, 9-10; 5:9-10
3. The flight of the army and the king	4-7	39:4-7; 52:8-11	1:3, 6; 2:2; 4: 19-20
4. The burning of the palace, Temple, and city	8-9	39:8; 52:13	2:3-5; 4:11; 5:18
5. The breaching of the city walls	10	33:4-5; 52:7	2:7-9
6. The exile of the populace	11-12	28:3-4, 14; 39:9-10	1:1, 4-5, 18; 2:9, 14; 3:2, 19; 4:22; 5:2
7. The looting of the Temple	13-15	51:51	1:10; 2:6-7
8. The execution of the leaders	18-21	39:6	1:15; 2:2, 20
9. The vassal status of Judah	22-25	40:9	1:1; 5:8-9
10. The collapse of the expected foreign help	24:7	27:1-11 37:5-10	4:17; 5:6

So significant is the destruction of Jerusalem that it is recorded four times in Scripture: 2 Kings 25; Jeremiah 39:1-
11; Jeremiah 52; and 2 Chronicles 36:11-21. The anguish
of that event could never be forgotten either in the depth of
its suffering or in the disturbing implications it seemed to
have for the eternal promises given in the history of salvation
up to that point in the Old Testament.

But it was necessary for the writer of Lamentations to

make those clear allusions to the historical events of those dreadful days of 587 B.C. Even if the suffering could not altogether be explained, it had to be located. Pent-up feelings of hurt and pain that were no longer linked to any datable event began to assume cosmic proportions. The unique became the all-consuming focus of one's attention. But should those feelings not be contained to that day, that month, year, or set of years in which the suffering took place? How could they be allowed to seep like ether into the whole fabric of life so that everything became tinted with the cloud of what should have been restricted and contained to a single act or series of events?

History is indeed extremely necessary; otherwise suffering will rule our whole lives and sorrow will carry us into the marsh of despondency, perhaps never to gain direction or purpose again. Eugene Peterson calls history the "anchor" and "ballast" needed to treat sorrow.[8] More than anything else a sense of balance, proportion, and location in the stream of history is basic. Only a separation from the historical memory of what caused our rejection, depression, alienation, hurt, and pain will permit that suffering to get out-of-hand. In this state of drifting, suffering often can be converted either into emotional problems, in which we get out of touch with reality, or a mere intellectual abstraction in which problems of theodicy or philosophies of the problem of pain become rational escapes and poor substitutes for facing the hurt and locating it in history.

The facts are recorded in 2 Kings 25 and Jeremiah 39 and 52. They are one long recital of the horrors and atrocities that came as a result of the siege and fall of Jerusalem along with all that came as its aftermath. The physical suffering alone was hard enough to chronicle, with such desperate scenes of starvation as women fighting over whose child was to be eaten next, women raped in Zion, and the princes hung by their hands in public execution.

But beyond the shame and grief of those obnoxious smells, sights, and sounds was the tale of the spiritual loss that was likewise being written in the same events. For this chosen people, chosen place, and chosen anointed king, it seemed to mean the end of every cherished hope of their salvation and calling of God.

How did so many come to lose so much in so little time? Could it be true that Jerusalem was the same city of which the psalmist had hymned: "Beautiful is her location, the joy of the whole earth" (Ps. 48:2)? Why did the psalmist ever dare write that the city of God was the "holy habitation of the Most High" or that "God is in the midst of her, she shall not be moved" (Ps. 46:4-5)?

But now the city, her walls, her towers, her palace, her homes, and even her temple were no more. Even the Davidic king, Zedekiah, "The breath of our nostrils, the anointed of the Lord" (Lam. 4:20) had been exiled and his sons executed before his very eyes. Gone also were the priests with the services of appointed feasts, sabbaths, the means of atonement, and the prophets with the living word of God. Even the land, the inheritance given by the Lord, was now owned and trampled by strangers.

All of this and more, Lamentations insists, must enter into the collective lament of God's people if its significance was ever to be found. History anchored sorrow and supplied the specific boundaries that were necessary to deal with it.

THE PLAN OF THE BOOK

In its external structure Lamentations exhibits an unusually fine artistic structure. First of all, there are five poems. Such an uneven number has the advantage of allowing one poem to signify the mid-point of the book if that is needed. And in fact that is what did happen; there is an "ascent" (*crescendo*) to a clearly marked climax in the third chapter. This third chapter is pivotal to the whole message of the book both in its form and content. Thus, the first two chapters form the "front steps" to the third chapter.

In fact, in chapter 3 we come to the darkest night of the sufferer's misery—"my splendor and all I had hoped from the Lord is gone" (v. 18).

> The poet could lay up in his heart everything that he had against God, but he could not shut God himself out of his heart. On the contrary it was proved, that after he had given the fullest expression to what he had in his heart against God, God himself was deeply rooted therein. The night was succeeded by the dawn of morning, as represented in vers. 19-21. With ver. 22, breaks the full day. From the beginning of the section, so full of hope and encouragement (ver. 22), the poet speaks in the plural number, as if he would make it most emphatically apparent, that this was common property. He continues to speak in the plural number till after the beginning of the third and last part of the song . . . [where] once more (ver. 48), the poet speaks in the singular number.[9]

Thus, there is an ascent to 3:22-44 and a descent from there to the final prayer in chapter 5.

This pivotal position of chapter 3 is also marked by an intensification of the acrostic, for only in this chapter do all twenty-two letters of the Hebrew alphabet occur three times in succession with every line in the stanza beginning with a letter of the alphabet in its sequence.

There is also a chiastic principle (a crisscross inversion such as *a-b, b-a*) in the external relations of the chapters. Chapters 1 and 5 are overall summaries of the disaster, chapters 2 and 4 are more explicit narratives of what took place, and chapter 3 occupies the central position. They appear, then, like this in narrating the tragedy:

Chapters: 1   2   3   4   5

Position: *a*   *b*   central   *b*   *a*

But in emotion, teaching, theological affirmation, and inner plan they move in this manner:

Chapters: 1   2   3   4   5

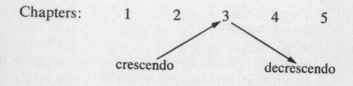

crescendo   decrescendo

The internal structure exhibits this tremendous ascent to the grand confession that "Great is [His] faithfulness: the Lord is my portion" (3:23-24). The path to this lofty ascent had begun by focusing on the city of Jerusalem in the first chapter. Its central plaintive cry is, "How deserted lies the *city!*" (1:1, italics added). There the poet spoke in the first person from verses 1-11 picturing the sad consequences of the sack and fall of Jerusalem in 587 B.C. In the second half of the chapter, Jerusalem, personified (a figure of speech where a thing, a quality, or an idea is represented as a person) as a woman, portrays her misfortunes and prays for help. The first chapter ends with a prayer in verses 20-22.

The second chapter concentrates on the *Temple* and Zion as God's dwelling place. Alas, we must also face divine anger in this chapter. The hallmark of the chapter again comes in the first verse: "How the Lord (note: not LORD, God's covenant name, but *Adonay*) has disgraced the daughter of Zion in His anger." Again, there is a three-fold development of this theme. The poet speaks and ascribes the destruction of Zion and the Temple to the agency of the Lord in verses 1-9. Then addressing personified Jerusalem in verses 10-19 the poet depicts the consequences of that destruction and urges her to pray. Finally, in verses 20-22 misery finds a voice and cries out in prayer.

The highest peak of the book is scaled in chapter 3. Here the suffering of an individual man appears. The speaker is the prophet himself as the representative of spiritual Israel. No doubt that speaker and prophet is Jeremiah himself, for he had suffered more than all the others and thus had plumbed both the depths of despair and the extremes of calamity. He had suffered not only from the Babylonians and the sad string of national reverses beginning with the tragic and senseless loss of the good young Davidic king, Josiah, in 609 B.C., but Jeremiah had also suffered at the hands of his own family, friends, and countrymen.

In three parts we move from the lament and hope of verses 1-24 to the bright sunlight of a meditation on the faithfulness and compassion of the Lord in verses 25-39. This is followed by a confession in verses 40-54 and a prayer in verses 55-60. The focal point is 3:22-24: "[It is a proof of] the gracious-love of the LORD that we are not consumed, for His compassions fail not; [they are] new every morning; great is Thy faithfulness. The LORD is my inheritance, says my soul; therefore I hope in Him."

The fourth lament (chapter 4) now relaxes the intensity of the emotional pitch of the earlier chapters and settles down to third-person speech. The sufferer has almost been drained of all strength and therefore the pace and tone must quiet down. This chapter focuses on how suffering has embraced all classes of the populace; chiefly, the nobles in verses 1-11 and the prophets and priests in verses 12-16. The last rays of hope fade in verses 17-22 as the Egyptians fail to come to their rescue, the Davidic king is taken prisoner, and Edom indulges in malicious joy over the whole sad turn of events.

The final chapter is a prayer, for it begins and ends with the petitions: "Remember, O LORD" and "Restore us . . . O LORD." Thus this last lament breaks out of the acrostic form (the *a, b, c* sequence is abandoned); it is much more succinct (there are only twenty-two lines), and it never uses the hollow *qinah* meter (a kind of "limping meter" in which the second of two parallel parts of the poetic stanza is one beat *shorter* than the first part, thereby creating a melancholy, incomplete feeling).

We may summarize the plan of the book in this manner:

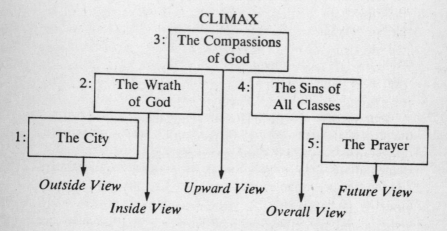

CLIMAX

3: The Compassions of God

2: The Wrath of God

4: The Sins of All Classes

1: The City

5: The Prayer

Outside View

Inside View

Upward View

Overall View

Future View

THE AUTHOR AND TIME OF COMPOSITION

No one is specifically named in the text as the author of Lamentations, but Jeremiah's name has been connected with this book by a very old tradition and by all commentators until this view was first challenged in 1712.

The Alexandrian form of the Greek Septuagint has these words preceding 1:1: "And it came to pass, after Israel had been carried away captive, and Jerusalem became desolate, that Jeremiah sat weeping, and lamented with this lamentation over Jerusalem, and said. . . ." The Latin Vulgate and the Arabic have these same words except the Vulgate adds before the final word "said" this phrase; "and with a sorrowful mind, sighing and moaning, he said. . . . " The Jewish Targum Jonathan simply begins by saying "Jeremiah the prophet and the chief priest [?] said. . . ."

The Talmud likewise regards Jeremiah as the author saying that "Jeremiah wrote his own book and the book of Kings and Lamentations."[10] This opinion is shared by Origen[11] and Jerome.[12]

The first to deny Jeremian authorship to the book of Lamentations was Herman von der Haardt in a 1712 commentary on the book in which he credited each of the five poems to Daniel, Shadrach, Meshach, Abednego, and King Jehoiachin respectively. Since that day it has become more and more fashionable to deny that Jeremiah penned these words in spite of the great amount of similarities in spirit, tone, language, and content shared with the book of Jeremiah.

There are five charges brought against the traditional view that Jeremiah wrote Lamentations.[13] They are: (1) an outright contradiction between 5:7 and Jeremiah 31:29-30, (2) Lamentations 2:14 proves the writer made use of Ezekiel, (3) the lack of emphasis on the sins of the people, (4) the artificiality of the acrostic form is atypical of Jeremiah, (5) many of the words and modes of expression do not occur in Jeremiah's prophecies. Each of these charges can be met with adequate evidence to the contrary.

Jeremiah's strong declaration that sons would not be put to death for their fathers' sin or fathers for their sons' sin (Jer. 31:29-30, a principle already in force in the Mosaic law of Deut. 24:16) was not meant to absolve from guilt those who had also sinned like their fathers. Lamentations 5:7 declared: "Our fathers sinned and are no more; and we bear their iniquities." The point was that the children *had* sinned exactly as their fathers had and so both bore the responsibility for their sins. Jeremiah had opposed the escapist mentality in the popular proverb (Jer. 31:29) that said "The fathers have eaten sour grapes and the children's teeth have been set on edge"—that is to say: "The old man sinned, so what am I to do? There is no sense in my repenting and trying to turn the favor of God toward us." How could the people of Judah claim their innocence or lay the blame solely at their fathers' feet?

Another objection to Jeremian authorship is found in Lamentations 2:14: "Your prophets have seen for you false and deceptive visions." It is true that the expression "to see a false vision" and the combination with "deceptive vision" occur nowhere else in the Old Testament except in Lamentations 2:14 and in Ezekiel (12:24; 13:6, 7, 8, 9, 10, 11, 14, 15, 23; 21:23, 29; 22:28). One other expression, "The perfection of beauty" or "she who is perfect in beauty" (Lam. 2:15) is used only in Ezekiel 27:3 of Tyre, in Ezekiel 28:12 of the king of Tyre, and in Psalm 50:2 of Zion. However, even though the vocabulary of Ezekiel 27:3 and 28:12 matches Lamentations 2:15, the context forces us to the Psalms since both refer to Jerusalem or Zion.

Likewise, the vocabulary in Lamentations 2:14 is Jeremian since Ezekiel uses the word we have translated "deceptive" in Lamentations 2:14 as meaning "Those who whitewash [things]" (Ezek. 13:10, 14, 15; 22:28), whereas the writer of Lamentations uses it in the metaphorical sense of "deceptive, absurd, or nonsense" just as Jeremiah had used a fuller spelling (*tiphlâh* instead of *taphēl*) of this same word meaning "absurdity" in Jeremiah 23:13 in reference to the false prophets of Samaria.[14] This is not to say that the writer of Lamentations may not have known Ezekiel and actually quoted from him in Lamentations 2:14. But such an admission for this one phrase is not enough to establish authorship especially for two writers who were near contemporaries.

The charge that sin is not emphasized in the laments is proved false by even a casual glance at 1:5, 8, 14, 18, 22; 2:14; 3:39, 42; 4:6, 13, and 5:7. The only great difference between Lamentations and the prophecy of Jeremiah is that

Jeremiah's task now is to comfort a severely chastised people; there is no need to warn that judgment is coming if they do not repent. And if it be said that passages such as Lamentations 1:4, 9, 19; 2:6, 9, 20, and 4:16 show a regard for ritual and the ceremonial law that were quite foreign to Jeremiah (presumably in passages like Jer. 7:21ff.), then we shall answer that modern readers have misunderstood Jeremiah's opposition to sacrifices and religious ritual. He insisted only on faith and obedience to God as the *prior condition* for worshiping and offering gifts to God. He did not reject the ritual aspects of the law.

The fourth complaint against a Jeremian authorship of this book is that any use of an alphabetic acrostic for four chapters (Lam. 1-4) is totally unlike Jeremiah, for he is too free and unorthodox in his approach to be bound by such an artificial form. But this charge assumes that the acrostic is a later, degenerate, and contrived work of art. Such an opinion cannot be sustained now that we are finding other laments, elegies (poems in praise or lament for the dead), and acrostics predating Lamentations by many centuries. One need only note the acrostics in Proverbs 31 and Psalms 25, 34, 37, and 145 to be aware that the argument has not been carefully framed. Moreover, the use of an alphabetic acrostic is most suitable for the soul's sustained pouring out of grief. Seldom had the human race been called upon to bear the load given that generation. Therefore, a unique event called for an unusual literary style.

Finally, it is true that the vocabulary and modes of expression of Lamentations are not the same as those of the prophecies of Jeremiah. Nägelsbach has given us a list of examples four pages in length.[15] However, Keil discounts "fully one-third of the words enumerated" since they ". . . are also found in the prophetic book of Jeremiah, though not quite in the same grammatical form. . . ."[16] Of the remaining words and expressions only five are used in any more than one poem even within Lamentations itself. Nägelsbach himself lays no stress on those words appearing only once; rather he stresses ". . . how may it be explained, that Jeremiah never uses *Elyon* or *Adonay* alone by itself, as a name of God, and yet that the latter occurs fourteen times in Lamentations. . . ."[17] The answer to the question is that both names for God are almost totally restricted to poetic address to God: *Elyon* (Lam. 3:35, 38) is used in the poetry of Numbers 24:16; Deuteronomy 32:8; Isaiah 14:14, and about twenty times in the Psalms; *Adonay* is used about forty times in the Psalms.

Furthermore, just as the prophecy of Jeremiah makes heavy use of Deuteronomy and the earlier prophets, so Lamentations makes heavy use of the Psalms and the book of Job. The best case for Jeremiah's authorship of these five elegies comes from four positive facts. First, Jeremiah was an acknowledged composer of laments, for 2 Chronicles 35:25 asserts: "Jeremiah composed laments for Josiah. . . . These became a tradition in Israel and are written in the Laments" (NIV). In spite of the contentions of a few,[18] Lamentations is not that collection referred to here, for Josiah's Laments are no longer extant. Second, Jeremiah was also the prophet who mourned, "Oh, that my head were a spring of water and my eyes a fountain of tears! I would weep day and night for the slain of my people" (Jer. 9:1, NIV). There is a strong presumption in favor of his being called to do just that from this prophetic word. Third, in Lamentations 3:1 the writer appears to identify himself with the prophet when he says, "I am the man who has seen affliction by the rod of His wrath." No other man could more rightfully lay claim to being chief sufferer than Jeremiah. Finally, add to this the long list of similarities in vocabulary, expressions, and subjects discussed in Lamentations and the poetical portions of Jeremiah and the case will be extremely persuasive.[19] Some of the key words, phrases, and ideas are:

	Lamentations	*Jeremiah*
1. "terrors on every side"	2:22	6:25; 20:3, 10; 46:5; 49:5, 29 [only in Ps. 31:13 elsewhere]
2. "My eyes flow with tears"	1:16; 2:18; 3:48	9:1, 18; 13:17; 14:17
3. "Wound" or "destruction"	2:11, 13; 3:47, 48 4:10	4:6, 20; 6:1, 14; 8:11, 21; 10:19; 14:17; etc.
4. "I have become the laughing-stock [of all the people]" hāyîtî śᵉḥoq in Lamentations hāyîtî liśᵉḥoq in Jeremiah	3:14	20:7
5. "terror and the pit"	3:47	48:43

We conclude that Jeremiah was the author of all five dirges in Lamentations and that he composed those poems shortly after the city of Jerusalem had fallen in 587 B.C., while the memory of the horrors was still fresh and vivid in his mind.[20] This final blow had climaxed a succession of swiftly moving events from 627 to 587 B.C. Not even Josiah's revival in 621 B.C. could contain the dreary string of reverses suffered by Israel. The writer of 2 Kings 23:26 felt obliged to explain this anamoly, that is, that revival and its accompanying righteousness did not in this case exalt the nation. The text cautions: "Nevertheless, [in spite of Josiah's revival] the LORD did not turn from the fierceness of His great anger . . . because of the provocations with which Manasseh [Josiah's grandfather who reigned from 693-639 B.C.] had provoked Him."

The greatest blow came when one of the finest kings Judah ever had, King Josiah, was killed at age thirty-nine by Pharaoh Necho in 609 B.C. Shortly after that, Babylon made its first incursion into the land and carried off among the choice captives Daniel and his three friends Meshach, Shadrach, and Abednego. An abortive rebellion in 597 B.C. led to another line of captives marching to Babylon including the prophet Ezekiel. But the final stroke came when Nebuchadnezzar returned in 587 B.C. and decimated the city, its palace, temple, homes, and people. Jerusalem had been besieged and starved into submission. King Zedekiah was captured in an attempted escape and witnessed the slaughtering of his sons before he lost his own sight at the hands of the Babylonians and was marched off to Babylon.

What was left? Gone was the city, "the joy of the whole earth." Gone was the glory of the Lord that had tabernacled in the Temple; only a burnt-out shell remained as a mute testimony against Judah's sins. Gone also were the princes, nobles, and the anointed Davidic king in whom all the promises of the everlasting plan of God's salvation for Israel and the whole earth rested. O, mournful day of unspeakable calamities!

THE TITLE AND PLACE IN THE CANON

Like the first five books of the Old Testament this book has no title in Hebrew and is therefore known by its first word *'êkâh,* an exclamatory (*not* an interrogative) particle meaning "How!" or "Alas!" This exclamation forms the initial word for three of the five dirges (1:1; 2:1; and 4:1). The Rabbis referred to this work by the nature of its contents, *qînôt,* "lamentations," and this became its title in the Talmud and Septuagint; the Greek translation of this term was *Threni* or *Threnoi* while the Vulgate and Latin writers translated it as *Lamenta.*

Other laments and funeral songs had preceded Jeremiah's. The longest and best example in Scripture is David's lament over Saul in 2 Samuel 1:17-27. Some briefer and more remote laments appear in Amos 5:1-2 (for the house of Israel), Ezekiel 19:1-14 (for the princes of Israel), Ezekiel 26:17-

21 and 27:2-9, 25-36 (for Tyre), and Ezekiel 28:11-19 (for the king of Tyre).

Two basic themes occur in the longer forms of *Leichen-lieden* (funeral songs); one is praise, the other is lament. The former praises the *past* glory of the deceased (the then) and the latter laments the sad state of the *present* (the now). This yields the schema of the *Einst und Jetzt* (the then and the now).

There are two traditional positions where Lamentations has appeared in the canon of the Old Testament. In the three-fold division of the Hebrew Bible (Law, Prophets, Writings) Lamentations was placed in the third division of the writings (*Ketûbîm*) under a section called the "Five Little Scrolls" (or *Megillôt*). This placement reflects the liturgical practice in the Jewish community in that they grouped together five of the shorter books that were used for public reading at the five important festivals in Israel. The Hebrew text used by scholars today is based on Codex Leningradensis, a copy dated to A.D. 1008 and housed in a Russian library in Leningrad. Its order is chronological:

Ruth
Song of Songs (when Solomon was young)
Ecclesiastes (when Solomon was old)
Lamentations
Esther

But in the Hebrew Bibles used by Askenazic Jews (the Jews who settled in middle and northern Europe after the Dispersion) the order follows the occurrence of the festivals on the calendar:

Song of Songs (Passover)
Ruth (Weeks, or Pentecost)
Lamentations (Ninth of Ab = destruction of Jerusalem)
Ecclesiastes (Succoth, i.e., Tabernacles)
Esther (Purim)

The second major tradition locates Lamentations after the

book of Jeremiah. This arrangement is used by the Septuagint (an ancient Greek translation of the third century B.C.) and the Vulgate and is followed by the English version. Josephus also knew of this order,[21] as did Melito of Sardis (d. A.D. 190),[22] Origen,[23] and Jerome.[24] Thus both locations have strong traditions and much depends on whether one emphasizes authorship or liturgical usage in determining the placement of Lamentations in the canon.

The importance of the book's place in the Old Testament canon rests in Jeremiah's carrying out of one of his functions as a prophet, namely his continued watch over the ruins of Jerusalem. Keil explains by saying:

> In these Lamentations he seeks not merely (1) to give expression to the sorrow of the people that he may weep with them, but by his outpour of complaint (2) to rouse his fellow-countrymen to an acknowledgment of God's justice in this visitation, (3) to keep them from despair under the burden of an unutterable woe, and (4) by teaching them how to give due submission to the judgment that has befallen them, (5) to lead once more to God those who would not let themselves be brought to Him through his previous testimony regarding that judgment while it was yet impending [numbering added].[25]

THE THEOLOGICAL AND PRACTICAL SIGNIFICANCE

> Nothing contrasts [the believing] and the humanist traditions more clearly than their respective responses to suffering. The modern humanist traditions see suffering as a deficiency—usually under the analogy of sickness. . . . Suffering, as such, has no value and no meaning—it is only a sign that things have gone wrong.[26]

The book of Lamentations is a book about suffering like the book of Job, but unlike Job it is closely linked to a national disaster. But it refuses merely to mark the fact that something has gone wrong. Suffering can only be a problem for those who believe that all the events of history are still under the hand of God. Therein lies the greatest obstacle and danger for believers: How can God's love and justice be reconciled with our pain? And if God's control of history is as complete as biblical faith claims it is, how did a nation like Israel ever suffer so much immediately after one of its most godly leaders (Josiah) led the people in such unprecedented revival in 621 B.C.? And where is God in the midst of some of earth's grimmest moments?

Lamentations will yield very few, if any, abstract or philosophical "answers" to the problem of suffering. Nevertheless, it will lead us into some very serious practical, theological reflections on the purposes and results of suffering. Instead of explaining pain, it helps us to face grief. In short, it is a pastoral tract that avoids the "cheery bromides" and offers "articulation" for one's suffering, "companionship" for support during the suffering,[27] and the seeds of hope (e.g., 3:20-36; 4:21-22; 5:19-21) for rebuilding one's life when the time has come for putting an end to the grief and pain left from the disaster.

Above all is the sufferer's encounter with God. Oftentimes He is the very one we had been avoiding only to have the silence of pain and the loneliness of suffering herd us back, as lost sheep, to the Shepherd of our souls. And if we are met with strong accents of God's love in the fact that He still cares enough to pursue us, albeit even if in suffering, we are also confronted with the bold fact of God's anger. Lamentations uses almost the full range of the Old Testament's rich and varied vocabulary for wrath.[28]

The book concludes with this haunting, but rhetorical question: "Have You [O LORD] utterly rejected us? Are You exceedingly angry with us?" (5:22). Yet it must be remembered that the question is asked in the context of prayer; therefore it assumes a personal, not an impersonal, relationship with God. Those who feel uncomfortable with all references in the Old Testament to God's anger or wrath should take heart, for "The moment anger is eliminated from

God, suffering is depersonalized. . . . Anger is an insistence on the personal—it is the antithesis of impersonal fate or abstract law."[29]

Probably the best contemporary discussion ever given to this problem of divine anger is to be found in the writings of Abraham J. Heschel. God, he explained,

> is . . . moved and affected by what happens in the world, and reacts accordingly. Events and human actions arouse in Him joy or sorrow, pleasure or wrath. He is not conceived as judging the world in detachment. He reacts in an animate and subjective manner and thus determines the value of events.[30]

Thus anger is God's sign that He still cares. It is the fabric out of which a more enduring friendship can be forged. Anger, as Peterson commented, "breaks through indifference. It smashes through apathy."[31] In the Old Testament, nouns for wrath are used 375 times for the wrath of God and only 80 times for that of men.[32] Furthermore,

> When a term for wrath is combined with a designation of God we usually find Yahweh. . . . The consistent linking of nouns for wrath with Yahweh, the covenant God, is of supreme theological significance. It shows that the idea of wrath is closely bound up with belief in the covenant.[33]

So God's anger is not despotic, unreasonable, or whimsical; it is related to violations of the covenant He made with His people and therefore, in a way, it is a sign that He has not abandoned either His people or His plan.

The use of God's covenant name Yahweh, used only with those who have a personal relationship with Him, is another clue that the wrath of Yahweh is something we should take personally.[34] In that personal relationship we again find that just as wrath came from the LORD (Yahweh), so now we find that He is full of "mercy and grace."

Another practical significance of these laments is their strong communal elements. Suffering has been transformed from private grief into an act of the whole community. Such communal participation protects us against "the threat of dehumanization to which all pain exposes us"[35] and guards against a depersonalization that can come from stubborn isolation. The involvement of the community of faith provides context to our grief and losses thereby making sure that pettiness, pride, and bitterness are not easy replacements for sorrow that has been denied her full course. Furthermore, every time the community joins my lament "sanction is given for the expression of loss—the outpouring of emotion is legitimized in such a way as to provide for catharsis [relieving of the emotions] and then renewal."[36]

Lamentations does teach us the language of prayer when we are in the midst of suffering. The basis of all such appeals to heaven is that the LORD can do something about conditions as they presently exist—*the now* must not be a prison with only *the then* of the past as a bromide to cheer us. The future can be different. Therefore, "Lift up your hands to Him for your children's lives" (2:19). With deep emotion and desperate importunity we are taught to make our complaints and sufferings known to the personal LORD of the covenant.

The focal point of the whole book comes in 3:22-24:

> The gracious love of the LORD never ceases,
> His compassions never fail;
> They are new every morning;
> Great is your faithfulness.
> "The LORD is my portion," I say to myself,
> Therefore I will hope in Him.

Here is the beacon of light among the ruins which resulted from Judah and Israel's covenant-breaking. Suddenly, under the deep affliction of suffering the community learns to express what Levi had confessed centuries ago, "The LORD is my portion" (cf. Num. 18:20; Deut. 10:9). With that confession came the realization that God's mercies and His covenantal love had not failed. In fact, His faithfulness was the greatest of all comforts and His compassion was evidenced anew every morning.

One further question may be faced here: Are some of the descriptions of Israel's suffering in Lamentations intended to be predictive of Christ's suffering on our behalf? Some claim that Christ is depicted as: (1) the one whom the LORD has afflicted (1:12), (2) the one who was mocked and despised by His enemies (2:15-16), (3) He who became the laughing-stock of all the people (3:14), (4) the one who was insulted and smote on His cheeks (3:30), (5) the weeping prophet par excellence (3:49-51; cf. Jesus weeping over Jerusalem in Matt. 23:37-38).

There is no clue given in the text that would support these claims other than the fact that there is a corporate solidarity between Israel as the "seed," "firstborn," and "my son" and the Messiah. This linkage of the One and the many, wherein the Old Testament writers deliberately chose terms that could refer equally well to that One who was to come and simultaneously to the whole group of believing Israel, is well attested in the Old Testament. This idea appears to be especially prominent in Lamentations where the office of the prophet personally and individually embodies the suffering that all Israel experienced in the events of 606 to 587 B.C. We shall leave this matter for a fuller discussion in the commentary, but items (1) and (2) in the above list would not appear to be justified by any fair interpretation of the text of Scripture.

COMPARISON WITH ANCIENT NEAR EASTERN LAMENTS

In the two millennia before Lamentations was composed there were numerous examples in the Near East of acrostic compositions. Adolf Erman has described several literary pieces from ancient Egypt that are a kind of acrostic in that all the stanzas have the same opening word.[37] In Mesopotamia a most elaborate acrostic from about 1000 B.C. has been found that, when the initial syllables of all the stanzas are taken together, spells out a sentence identifying the writer and his loyalty to the god and king.[38]

Although it is true that these are syllable or word acrostics and not alphabetic acrostics as in the Old Testament, we still contend that the basic idea of utilizing a pattern of syllables, words, or letters that in one way stood outside the content of the composition and in another way were intimately connected with the substance of the literary piece is well attested outside Hebrew literature and is no necessary reason for late-dating a piece or denying its authenticity. Even the confusion aroused by the apparent reversal of the letters *ayin* and *pe* (approximately *o* and *p* in our alphabet) in Lamentations 2, 3, and 4 can now be authenticated in older Canaanite alphabets. In Ugaritic (the language of a Canaanite coastal city that was at its height from the fifteenth to the twelfth centuries B.C.) abecedaries, *pe* comes before *ayin* in their alphabet as it does in Lamentations 2, 3, and 4.

Although there was no *direct* influence on the biblical writer of Lamentations it is clear that there were a number of Sumerian and Akkadian lamentations for cities. Some examples are: "The Lamentation over the Destruction of Ur," "Lamentation over the Destruction of Sumer and Ur," "Lamentation over the Destruction of Nipper," and "The Second Lamentation for Ur."[39]

Few people would want to argue that a second millennium Mesopotamian composition was the source of a fifth century B.C. biblical book, but there are one or two similarities that are nonetheless interesting in that they treat themes common to both literary worlds because the experiences are similar.

ANET p. 618: lines 403-4	Lam. 1:20c
Ur . . . *inside* it we die of *famine*	*Outside* the sword killed my children
Outside it we are killed by the weapons of the Elamites	*Inside,* it was *famine*

(But note already the parallels in Deuteronomy 32:25, Jeremiah 14:18, and Ezekiel 7:15).[40]

ANET p. 651: lines 254-55	Lam. 5:18
Over your *usga* (?)—place established for lustrations	On mount Zion, which lies desolate
May the "fox of the ruined mounds" glide (his) tail	Foxes prowl about.

The same criticism may be raised about this parallel. Ruined cities routinely became the haunts of wild animals. Scripture is replete with warnings and illustrations of this phenomenon. It is also found in more contemporary literature in the Near East—even if it is not in the lament form. So what we are dealing with is not a case of literary borrowing but a fact of life and an associated proverbial truth that grew out of that fact of life.[41]

THE POETIC STRUCTURE OF LAMENTATIONS

Up to now, Hebrew poetry has been characterized by its distinctive emphasis on a balancing of ideas between the lines (called Hebrew Parallelism) rather than as possessing a distinctive rhythmic pattern. In fact, to this very day no one school can convince the other that it has discovered the proper formula for defining Hebrew poetic meter. Some believe that the meter can be determined by watching the stressed and unstressed syllables (Hölscher, Mowinckel, Horst, Segert). Others argue that the key is accents and not Hebrew syllables (Ley, Sievers), and still others stress the number of syllables per line (Freedman). The truth is, no one knows. It may well be that Hebrew poetry does not have any meter (G. D. Young).

But Hebrew poetry does possess parallelism (balance of ideas). Even here we are disappointed to learn that Hillers found that 104 out of 266 lines in Lamentations (or 39 percent) exhibited no form of parallelism[42] (unless it be what some scholars call synthetic or formal parallelism, that is, the lines are placed side by side as if the complete sentence they form had a break between and as if the parallel line contrasted or repeated the idea of the opening line with different terms as it does in antithetical or synonymous parallelism).[43] Hillers stated that only 3 of the 22 lines in the prayer of chapter 5 had no parallelism. Yet in the first four chapters 41 percent contained no semantic or grammatical resemblance between the lines of the strophe (poetic paragraph; e.g., Lam. 1:2*b*).[44] The important point of all this discussion is simply this: Where Hebrew parallelism is absent or not apparent it becomes extremely difficult, if not impossible at times, to decide syntactically where the line division (*caesura*) comes. This will affect any commentary to some extent, and it should be frankly admitted by all commentators.

The pioneer study on the meter and poetic structure of Lamentations appeared in a German journal article written in 1882 by Karl Budde.[45] Budde made one key contribution that has tended to stand. He named the hollow or limping kind of verse that tends to be associated with poems of lament: *qinah* meter. In the *qinah* pattern the first poetic line is at least one word longer than the second line giving the most typical pattern of 3 + 2, but also of 4 + 3 and 4 + 2. For example, in Lamentations 3:4-5 the typical 3 + 2 pattern appears this way (hyphenated words represent one Hebrew word):

	1	2	3
4.	He - wore - out	my - flesh	and - my - skin

	1	2	3
	He - broke	my - bones	. . . .

	1	2	3
5.	He - has - besieged	and - encircled	around - me

	1	2	3
	with - bitterness	and - hardship	. . . .

The effect that the missing third element in the second line creates is one of hollowness and a limping gait. It is like waiting for the other shoe to fall—only it never does. This format adds to the dark mood and heavyheartedness of the poet as he matches the poetic form to the content being treated.

THE CHRISTIAN USE OF LAMENTATIONS

One final remark might help set the tone for our study of Lamentations. Suffering, grief, and pain are familiar if unwelcomed visitors to most lives. Oftentimes the believer has not been aided or prepared by solid exposition of Scripture or a theology of suffering to cope with the suffering as it comes in national disaster, death, depression, separation, rejection, or the like. Too frequently the only place many turn in such circumstances is to medically trained clinicians. This is not to say that a referral to the medical profession is not altogether appropriate at times; but we do maintain that "grief management," as the phrase goes these days, is the business of the gospel as well.

Instead of sporting techniques, answers, or slogans, Lamentations supplies: (1) orientation, (2) a voice for working completely through grief (from *a* to *z*), (3) instruction on how and what to pray, and (4) a focal point in God's faithfulness and in the fact that He is our portion. Is that not what we need in the midst of trouble and calamity? Surely comfort, community, compassion, companionship, and conclusion to suffering are all found in this marvelous little book inserted in the biblical corpus for people and times like ours.

NOTES

1. Eugene H. Peterson, *Five Smooth Stones for Pastoral Work* (Atlanta: John Knox, 1980), p. 96.
2. Of the thirteen acrostics in the Old Testament, Lamentations 1-4 and Psalm 119 are the longest. The others are found in Proverbs 31:10-31; Psalms 9-10, 25, 34, 37, 111, 112, 145.
3. There is no evidence that the acrostic was used because of some original belief in its magical power.
4. Peterson, p. 97. See also Norman K. Gottwald, *Studies in The Book of Lamentations* (London: SCM, 1962), pp. 28-32.
5. Two possible exceptions to this rule are Lamentations 1:7 and 2:19, which appear to have four lines.
6. Peterson, p. 101.
7. This list was suggested in part by Norman K. Gottwald, "Lamentations, Book of," in *The Interpreter's Dictionary of the Bible*, 4 vols. and supplement, ed. George A. Buttrick, (New York: Abingdon, 1962), 3:62.
8. Peterson, p. 103.
9. C. W. Eduard Nägelsbach, *The Lamentations of Jeremiah*, trans., enlarged, and ed. William H. Hornblower in *Lange's Commentary on the Holy Scriptures*, 25 vols. (New York: Scribner, Armstrong, 1870), vol. 8, p. 4.
10. *Baba Bathra*, 15:1.
11. See Eusebius's *Ecclesiastical History*, 4:25.
12. Jerome "Prologus Galeatus," *Patrologia Latina*, 28 vols. 28:cols. 593-604; Zechariah 12:11.
13. This list depends heavily upon C. F. Keil in C. F. Keil and F. Delitzsch, *The Prophecies of Jeremiah: Biblical Commentary on The Old Testament*, 25 vols. (Grand Rapids: Eerdmans, 1956), 20:341-50.
14. For fuller argumentation, see Keil, pp. 342-45.
15. Nägelsbach, pp. 10-14.
16. Keil, 20:347.
17. Nägelsbach, p. 13.
18. Josephus (*Antiquities of the Jews*, 10.5.1) thought the fourth chapter of Lamentations related to King Josiah, but that chapter concerns a city and its classes of people.
19. For this list, see Edward J. Young, *Introduction to the Old Testament* (Grand Rapids: Eerdmans, 1953), pp. 333-36. Also see Keil, 20:349. For an extended and masterful advocacy of Jeremian authorship, see W. H. Hornblower's "Additional Remarks" in *Lange's Commentary*, pp. 19-35.
20. This almost unanimous view among scholars has one exception. Wilhelm Rudolph in 1962 argued that Lamentations 1 must date from the 597 B.C. invasion by the Babylonians when Ezekiel was taken captive since that chapter makes no reference to the destruction of the city or Temple. But as Delbert Hillers warns, "This is essentially an argument from silence." *Lamentations: The Anchor Bible* (Garden City, N.Y.: Doubleday, 1972), p. xix.
21. Josephus *Contra Apionem*, 1:8.
22. Eusebius *Ecclesiastical History*, 4:26:14.

23. Ibid., 6:25:2.
24. Jerome 28: cols. 593-604.
25. Cf. Keil, 20:351-352.
26. Peterson, p. 111.
27. Words suggested by Peterson, p. 110.
28. Wesley J. Fuerst, *The Cambridge Commentary: The Books of Ruth, Esther, Ecclesiastes, The Song of Songs, Lamentations: The Five Scrolls* (Cambridge: Cambridge U., 1975), p. 45.
29. Peterson, p. 106.
30. Abraham J. Heschel, *The Prophets,* 2 vols. (New York: Harper & Row, 1971), 2:4.
31. Peterson, p. 108.
32. Johannes Fichtner, "The wrath of God," *Theological Dictionary of the New Testament,* ed. Gerhard Friedrich, trans. and ed. Geoffrey W. Bromiley, 10 vols. (Grand Rapids: Eerdmans, 1967), 5:395, n. 92.
33. Ibid., p. 396.
34. Peterson, p. 109.
35. Ibid., p. 115.
36. Ibid.
37. Adolf Erman, *The Ancient Egyptians,* trans. A. M. Blackman (New York: Harper & Row, 1966), pp. lviii-lix. Originally translated and published in English under the title *The Literature of the Ancient Egyptians* (London: Methuen & Co., 1927).
38. W. G. Lambert, *Babylonian Wisdom Literature* (Oxford: Oxford U., 1960), pp. 63-68. For much later developments, see Ralph Marcus, "Alphabetic Acrostics in the Hellenistic and Roman Periods," *Journal of Near Eastern Studies* 6 (1947), pp. 109-15.
39. Samuel Noah Kramer, "Sumerian Literature and the Bible," *Studia Biblica et Orientalia,* III: *Oriens Antiquus,* Anelecta Biblica, 12 (Rome: 1959). Also see Samuel N. Kramer in James Pritchard, ed., *Ancient Near Eastern Texts Relating to the Old Testament* 3d ed. (Princeton: Princeton U., 1969), pp. 455-63.
40. The examples and criticism are from Hillers, p. xxx.
41. For a stronger protest, see T. F. McDaniel, "The Alleged Sumerian Influence Upon Lamentations," *Vetus Testamentum* 18 (1968), pp. 198-209. He finds nothing compelling in these alleged parallels except the common subject matter of grief on the occasion of the fall of a city.
42. Hillers, p. xxxiv.
43. For further discussion, see Walter C. Kaiser, Jr., *Toward an Exegetical Theology: Biblical Exegesis for Preaching and Teaching* (Grand Rapids: Baker, 1981), pp. 211-31.
44. Hillers, p. xxxiv.
45. Karl Budde, "Das hebräische Klagelied," *Zeitschrift für die alttestamentliche Wissenschaft* 2 (1882), pp. 1-52.

1

Coping with Grief

The first of the five Lamentations has one monotonous theme repeated five times: "There is no one to comfort (*'ên m⁰naḥēm*—1:2, 9, 16, 17, 21). In this exceptionally vivid depiction of the desolation of Zion, the city of God, this one phrase rings like the heavy gong of a funeral bell. But another note of gloom is struck in a related word in Lamentations 1:3, "she finds no rest." The word for "rest"(*manôaḥ*) is related in Hebrew to the word for "comfort" (*m⁰naḥēm*) and is a word possessing considerable theological weight. The "rest" of God is a state of being that we enter into by belief. Note that in Hebrews 3:17—4:2 the Israelites who wandered in the desert with Moses failed to enter into that same "rest," which is being offered to us today, because they did not receive the "good news" or "gospel" by faith. But rest was also the promised land God pledged to the patriarchs.[1]

Jerusalem is personified as a woman who has been forsaken by her friends, massacred by her enemies, left bereft of her former glory, and now stands comfortless and without any "resting place." Zion in her stateless, friendless, hopeless, godless, and Messiahless condition was without a "resting place;" her condition was the reverse situation of the Moabitess, Ruth, who found a place of rest in Jehovah and Judah (Ruth 1:9; 3:1).

Modern readers must not view this chapter in a detached and disinterested way, for there is an implied warning here. To use the question of Luke 23:31, "If this is what was done to the green tree, what will happen to the dry?" If God has done this to the people He called the "apple of His eye" (Deut. 32:10), what will He do to the nations and peoples of the world today? Nägelsbach correctly answers: "Truly, since the Lord could destroy Jerusalem and entirely lay waste Canaan, without being unfaithful to His promise given to the Fathers, even so He can remove the candlestick of every particular Christian church, without breaking the promise given to the church at large, that the gates of Hell shall not prevail against it (Matt xvi.18)."[2]

Nägelsbach points out one additional lesson that we may gain from this chapter.[3] In contrast to the stoical philosophies of the heathen, which demand that wise and intelligent men and women should be altogether emotionless, never rejoicing when there is good news or despondent when there is misfortune, Jeremiah teaches us in Lamentations 1 that such emotions, properly controlled, are not obnoxious to God. He, in fact, planted the ability for such emotions in us. Romans 12:15 commands us in the ordinary affairs of life to rejoice with those who rejoice and weep with those who weep. Steeling oneself against the misfortunes of life may lead to a heart of bitterness, revenge, and permanent loneliness.[4] Weep, then, we must.

THE STANZAS IN LAMENTATIONS 1

Based on the use of the third- and first-person pronoun we may divide the chapter (with almost all commentators) into two main parts: verses 1-11 and 12-22. Both parts are closely connected. It would appear that emotional and psychological progress is realized in this poem as it moves from a more distant, descriptive third-person reporting in verses 1-11 to a more personal, private first-person speech in verses 12-22.[5]

In the first section the poet speaks on behalf of Jerusalem, who is personified as a woman. Her present state is sharply contrasted with what she once was (vv. 1-3). Her forsaken roads, abandoned gates, grieving priests and maidens, exiled princes and nobles all tell part of her sad story (vv. 4-7). The reason for this wretched state of affairs (already hinted at in verse 5) is her awful sin (vv. 8-9), which we may divide off into a separate sub-section of verses 8-11. Even her sanctuary has been decimated (v. 10) and her young children traded for food during the harsh famine (v. 11). Two heavy first-person sighs interrupt this description of her misery (vv. 9c and 11c).

The second section shifts to the first-person pronoun and now Jerusalem speaks for herself as she has already done momentarily in verses 9c and 11c. This section may be divided into two equal parts, however, since the complaint of verses 12-16 ends suddenly when the poet once again intrudes for just a moment in verse 17 to repeat and confirm what Zion has just said. But when Zion resumes her speech in verse 18 she confesses that the LORD had been in the right all along and that she had sinned (vv. 18-22). Thus we may divide verses 12-22 into a complaint (vv. 12-16) and a confession (vv. 18-22), with verse 17 being transitional.

THE FOCAL POINT OF LAMENTATIONS 1

If the fivefold repetition of the phrase "there is no comfort" supplies not only the tone but also the subject of this chapter, where does the passage come to some kind of focus? What concept, word, or verse will act for this passage as the center of a circle does for its circumference? Where may we put the point of the compass so it will embrace all the contents of the chapter?

We believe verse 18 is that focal point, for on this verse pivots not only this chapter but any use made of this chapter for teaching or preaching. Jeremiah 12:1 had exclaimed in similar words and now verse 18 declares: "The LORD is in the right [with the unexpressed ellipsis 'and we are in the wrong'] for [we] have rebelled against His word" (literally "His mouth"). That seems to say it all.

The same confession was made, albeit with mental reservations, by Pharaoh: "The LORD is in the right, and I and my people are in the wrong" (Exod. 9:27). Ezra prayed on behalf of Israel and confessed: "O Lord, the God of Israel, you are in the right . . . behold, we are before you in our guilt" (Ezra 9:15). The people of Israel acknowledged "You are in the right with respect to all that has come on us, for you have acted faithfully whereas we have behaved wickedly" (Neh. 9:33).

In spite of the heavy weight of suffering and pain laid on the city of Jerusalem by the LORD, Jerusalem's and Judah's confession, like ours, must be that the LORD is always "right," "just," and "righteous" in all His ways. No doubt the informing theology of a passage like Deuteronomy 32:4 ("all His ways are right, a God of faithfulness and without sin; just and right is He") lies behind this confession.

Had she listened to the word spoken from the "mouth of God" Zion would never have experienced the horror and nightmare of suffering she now found herself in. We too at the end of our study of this chapter ought to come to the same conclusion; rebellion against God's Word is downright foolishness—individually and nationally. Every act of God is right, for He is altogether righteous and just in all He directs and all He permits.

A TEACHING OUTLINE FOR LAMENTATIONS 1

Coping with Grief

Key word: *Elements* (of grief)

1. In Its Loneliness   1:1-7
2. In Its Causes   1:8-11
3. In Its Purposes   1:12-17
4. In Its Confession   1:18-22

EXPOSITION AND APPLICATION

In a world filled with so much sorrow and pain men and women—especially believers—must cope with grief. But how? Jeremiah, under the inspiration of the Spirit of God, would aid us in coping just as he aided himself and the grieving Jewish community on the heels of one of the greatest tragedies ever to befall Israel. In one of the most tear-filled chapters of the five in Lamentations, Israel (and the believing community through the centuries) was taught about *coping with grief.*

1. *In its loneliness* (1:1-7). In these seven verses the poet speaks in the third person on behalf of the city of God—troubled Jerusalem. Part of the healing process in working through tragedy in all its forms is the act of pouring out our complaint to God. The context for this poem is one of supplication to God (see vv. 9c, 11c, 18-22). Thus we are taught to pour out our complaint, sorrow, and anguish to the God in whose presence we not only live but also suffer.

Yet this is so hard because we sense such a total alienation from God. How can mortals in their state of feeling cut off, abandoned, and lonely address God in prayer? Where does one begin?

The text begins by encouraging us to "tell it like it is," to explain our loneliness in all its gruesome and boring (to everyone except our Lord) details. In this chapter loneliness can be itemized in the following:

> The Loss of Abundance (v. 1)
> The Loss of Allies (v. 2)
> The Loss of a Resting Place (v. 3)
> The Loss of Happiness (v. 4)
> The Loss of Prestige (v. 5)
> The Loss of Courage (v. 6)
> The Loss of Worship (v. 7).

No wonder the text begins in 1:1 by exclaiming, "How!" (*'ekâh*). This ejaculatory word was used on numerous occasions in the biblical text for laments and funeral songs. The effect was to express astonishment, sorrow, or indignation much like the vernacular "Good grief!" or the Yiddish *oiee*

Vaah! It is used this way in Isaiah 1:21—"How the faithful city has become a harlot"; 14:4—"How the oppressed has ceased"; Jeremiah 9:19—"How we are ruined"; 48:17—"How the mighty scepter is broken"; Ezekiel 26:17—"How you have vanished"; and later in Lamentations 2:1 and 4:1.

In fact, the prophet appears to have Isaiah 1:21 in mind for in both passages Jerusalem is the subject. She is treated as if she were a real person (personified) in that the text uses the third-person singular feminine pronoun for its verbs or suffixes on nouns (*she* weeps, *her* cheeks, *her* tears, *her* foes) and she is plainly called a "widow" in verse 1. Thus, not the collection of the exiled people but the city of Jerusalem is the widow the prophet now mourns as she sits alone beside the desecrated holy place where once the Lord dwelt.

The shame of the whole matter is found in what she *once was* and what Jerusalem *is now* (v. 1):

> *once* full of people—*now* sitting alone
> *once* great among the nations—*now* a widow
> *once* queen of the cities—*now* a slave.

Verse three extends this contrast, but by personifying Judah; *once* Judah dwelt as an independent nation—*now* she has gone into exile.[6]

And as if all this were not enough the most doleful note of all epitomizes this chapter: "She has none to comfort her" (vv. 2, 9, 16, 17, 21). We are not surprised, then, to find that this chapter is filled with so many tears. Constantly "she weeps bitterly" with a stream of "tears on her cheeks" (vv. 2, 16), "she groans" (vv. 8, 21, 22), and her "eyes flow with tears" (v. 16), for she is "in distress" and "turmoil of soul" and "her heart is wrung out in her" (v. 20).

A third personage is introduced in verses 4-7: Zion. This ideal person is not the *city*, described in all her former glory in verses 1-2, or the *nation* Judah, once an independent state among the family of nations (v. 3), but the *place where Jehovah dwells*. Strictly speaking, Zion was the hill on which the Temple was built, but later on it came to be applied to the whole city.

What had happened to the city and nation had now overtaken the religious center and life of this people—Zion. Gone were the days of the crowded roads with pilgrims making their way to Jerusalem for the wonderful festivals and solemn assemblies. Gone too were the gates, not of Jerusalem in this instance, but of the sacred precincts; the holy place had lost its sanctity. Both priests and virgins heaved heavy sighs—the leaders of Israel's religious life and the promise for the future generation.

Now for the first time the name of Jehovah (Yahweh) is introduced in connection with Zion. He it was who had afflicted Zion because of the magnitude of her sin. Thus already the poet anticipates verses 8-10 and the whole of chapter 2. But the fact remained, as the prophets had warned so frequently, that God had once again used a foreign nation as His instrument of punishment because of accumulated sin of a nation (vv. 8, 18, 20, 22). As a result, "her children have been taken captive" and "all her beauty is gone" (i.e., the presence of and worship of the Lord Ps. 96:9; Ezek. 9:3; 10:19; 11:22; 43:5).

Verse 7 summarizes the whole section and suddenly for the first time the name *Jerusalem* appears as the generic or comprehensive term that incorporates all that is the widow (the *city*), Judah (the *nation*), and Zion (the *center of worship*). The accent is on her utter helplessness as her enemies mocked and laughed at her deep misery. All she could do was to remember the former days of happiness. Meanwhile, her adversaries "made a mockery of her sabbaths." Keil is no doubt correct when he comments:

> The mockery of enemies does not apply to the Jewish celebration of the Sabbath . . . but to the cessation of the public worship of the Lord, inasmuch as the heathen, by destroying Jerusalem and the temple, fancied they had not only put an end to the worship of the God of the Jews, but also

had conquered the God of Israel as a helpless national deity, and made a mock[ery] of Israel's faith in Jahweh as the only true God.[7]

2. *In its causes* (1:8-11). It is not always necessary or even desirable to probe one's past for all the root causes of pain and suffering, but when we come to realize that *some* forms of suffering are retributive and are connected with previous sin nothing will assuage our pain or allow us to cope with grief until we acknowledge our guilt and repeated transgressions. Our passage lists four such causes:

> The shame sin brings (v. 8)
> The defilement sin brings (v. 9)
> The desecration sin brings (v. 10)
> The famine sin brings (v. 11).

Few things were more humiliating to a person in the ancient Near East than to be stripped of all clothing. Such exposure was reserved for punishing prostitutes (Ezek. 16:35-39; 23:29) and metaphorically it is used as punishment for nations (Isa. 47:3; Ezek. 16:37; Hos. 2:10; Nah. 3:5; Lam. 4:21).

When all of Jerusalem's innermost recesses had been violated it was plain that her lack of morality had likewise been unmasked. It was exactly as Nebuzaradan, the captain of the Babylonian guard who released Jeremiah from the exiles headed for Babylon, said: "The Lord has brought about and done as He said because [Judah] sinned against the Lord and did not obey His voice. [Therefore] this thing has come upon you" (Jer. 40:3).

Moreover, what Judah and we sometimes fail to realize is that the longer we trifle with sin the more certain it is that in the end the "filthiness" will show up on our clothes (v. 9). One day it will no longer be possible to hide our guilt. How thoughtless of humanity to "take no thought of [their] doom!" That is exactly what Moses had warned in Deuteronomy 32:29, "If they [and we] were wise . . . they [and we]

would think of our latter end." Even Babylon had been held
to the same obligation—she thought she would always remain a mistress and she did not think of the end or outcome
of all her sins (Isa. 47:7). As for the end—it came just as
"wondrously" (even "miraculously") as did her deliverance
from Egypt: "her fall was astounding."[8]

Another cause of Jerusalem's grief was the desecration of
her Temple. Nägelsbach observes, "Since [Jerusalem] has not
preserved the sanctuary of her heart from pollution by the
enemy of her soul, but has [allowed] that enemy to rob her
of her spiritual treasures, she must not wonder if her earthly
enemies desecrate by their presence her earthly sanctuary
and stretch out the hand towards its precious things."[9] The
Gentiles, who had been forbidden even to worship with the
congregation of Israel (of Ammon and Moab in Deut. 23:
3-4; extended to all nations in Neh. 13:3; Ezek. 44:7, 9),
had entered into the *holy place* itself—a place where only
the priests could enter!

One more cause for sorrow can be added to this list of
horrors: hunger. Valuables and jewels must now be exchanged for the most meager of subsistence, so great was the
physical hunger and famine of the people in the land. If the
priests groaned and sighed in verse 4 and the city of Jerusalem in verse 8, now all the people join in that sigh as they
search for bread.

Twice in this section a most earnest supplication born out
of the direst of circumstances goes up to God: "O LORD,
look and consider" (vv. 9, 11; cf. also 1:20; 2:20; 5:1).

3. *In its purposes* (1:12-17). The second half of this
lament intensifies as the plan and purposes of the Lord are
unveiled. Jerusalem herself will now speak for almost the
entirety of the remaining portion of the chapter as she describes the exceptional nature of her pain. Those who are
uninvolved in her pain and who are mere passersby—sort
of "everyman"—will be asked rhetorically to look, listen, and
compare Jerusalem's grief to that which any of them have

ever experienced.[10] This is not too much different from what we also do in our grief. We believe what we are going through is extraordinary and totally removed from what any normal human being can bear.

But through it all Jerusalem can still map out for our profit the purposes that Yahweh had in putting her through this experience. They include these reasons:

> To turn us back to the Lord (v. 13)
> To tie us up in our sin (v. 14)
> To crush us before our enemies (v. 15).

In verses 13-15 Jerusalem describes under four strong metaphors the sufferings she endured: fire that fell from heaven, the hunter's net spread to trap wild animals, the animal yoke fastened to the neck of a man, and the tramping out and crushing of grapes in the winepress. In one way or another each of these images depicts the *dies irae,* a day of wrath belonging to the Lord. The fire that falls from heaven is actually from God Himself, for heaven is only a round-about way of saying the same thing (See Gen. 19:24; 2 Kings 2:10, 12, 14; Ps. 11:6). Likewise the imagery of God spreading the net as a snare to trap or check a man's walk or lifestyle can be found in Psalm 94:13; Jeremiah 50:24; Ezekiel 12:13; 17:20; 32:3; Hosea 7:12. Even the figure of the yoke was dramatized during Jeremiah's ministry when he built and wore successively a wooden and iron yoke much to the consternation of the false prophet Hananiah in Jeremiah 28. The winepress is also a symbol of final judgment in Isaiah 63:1-4 and Revelation 14:18-20; 19:13-15. Already Joel 3:13 and Jeremiah 6:9 had used this imagery as a symbol of God's judgment on the magnitude of the wickedness of Israel.

The emphasis of these verses appears, however, to fall on God's purposes in suffering of this kind. Was it not, as Jerusalem confessed in verse 13, "He turned me back [to Himself]"?[11] One of the great Old Testament words for repentance is this word for "turn" (*šub*). It calls for a total reversal of one's field; a 180 degree turnaround to face God and His purposes.

The second purpose grief worked is announced in verse 14: transgression had imposed its yoke on the neck until it had made Jerusalem's strength fail. Thus sins, like a yoke, had become tangled together until they had reached up to the neck and had broken all strength. Unchecked sin can so bind its practitioners that all power to overcome it or the grip of those into whose hand such sinners eventually fall is spent and gone. Only by reducing sinners to such desperate straits will some eventually listen and turn. Thus grief may often work a very wonderful work that none of the goodness or blessings of God will ever effect.

The last purpose of God is seen when He often must take the sickle and begin to harvest the grapes so that He may place them in the winepress to be trampled, pressed, crushed, and squeezed for the making of wine. Again, this pressing and bruising is His doing. By it He wants to accomplish special purposes that He could not perform in us in any other way. Fortunately enough it is He who treads the winepress, therefore the "virgin daughter of Zion" may expect the most merciful and kindest treatment.

Nevertheless, the pain is hard (v. 16) and the "comforter," even though He works His purposes, still seems miles away. Jerusalem returns in verse 16 to the unprecedented sorrow that she had expressed as she began this section in verse 12.

For a brief moment Jeremiah interrupts to corroborate her analysis of things. Indeed, Jerusalem is without any human comforter, for Yahweh has so ordered it. All her neighbors, some who were even recent allies, are now all hostile antagonists and are aware of her exposed defilement (vv. 8-9).

4. *In its confession* (1:18-22). The brief interlude of verse 17 has provided us with a suitable pause. It is almost

as if the flow of tears had momentarily choked off any further lamentation for the city and reminded Jerusalem how vain it was to spread forth her hands to all who passed by. What was the use? Yahweh had ordered it, therefore it was to Him that she must go.

Thus in one magnificent moment of bravery and honesty Jerusalem confesses her sin to the Lord and makes her entreaties to Him as she had begun to do in verses 9c and 11c. Her confessions and entreaties are these:

> The Lord has been in the right (v. 18a)
> We have rebelled against His word (vv. 18b-19)
> We plead for Him to witness our sufferings (v. 20)
> We plead for His requital of our enemies (vv. 21-22).

If verses 5 and 17 establish that the Lord is the one who has directed or permitted suffering in this city, then verse 18 declares that He has been more than justified in what He has done. Jeremiah had learned the same truth in his own suffering: "You are in the right, O LORD, whenever I lodge my complaint with you . . ." (Jer. 12:1).

The unexpressed form of the ellipsis here (as we mentioned above under the focal point of the chapter) is [". . . and we are in the wrong"]. In fact, Jerusalem confesses even more openly: "I have rebelled against your word [literally 'your mouth']." The same expression appears in Numbers 20:24; 27:14 and 1 Kings 13:21, 26. With this double acknowledgement the highest point in this prayer has been reached and the greatest step toward coping with grief had been mastered.

Once more as in verse 12 Jerusalem calls on the nations to listen and witness her deep sorrow. As this kind of disaster and pain has a habit of doing, the recent holocaust then floods into her mind again and she instinctively seeks human sympathy. Four of these hurts are listed again: (1) she has lost her pride (virgins) and strength (young men) in the captivity, (2) her lovers (allies, as also in Lam. 1:2

and Jer. 30:14) have proven unreliable, (3) her officials in the city and the Temple are now dead, (4) there was no food for those in high places, much less the commoner. But this apostrophe or turning to the nations (v. 18) as well as to the passersby (v. 12) is probably more of a poetic turn to express the extent and weight of her grief and sorrow.

Even so, there was no help from men—just as there has not been all along. This former queen of all the cities of the earth *must* turn now to the Lord and to Him alone. The first appeal in verse 20 is for our Lord to witness the great mental and emotional state of agitation the sufferer is in as a result of what she has experienced. The *New International Version* renders verse 20*a-b* well: "See, O LORD, how distressed I am! I am in torment within, and in my heart I am disturbed, for I have been most rebellious." The "strait" (*sar*) or difficulty was her deep distress and the commotion of her "bowels" (literally) was her "torment" (NIV) or "severe mental agitation." Even her "heart was overturned within her," an experience God shared in another setting in Hosea 11:8.

But the reasons were all of her own doing—she had rebelled most grievously. Accordingly, no place inside or out was safe; both reeked of either the sword or death.

The second and final request is that the Lord might move in requital against the jeering and leering nations. The verb in verse 21 is "they heard" instead of an imperative as the first word was in verse 20. It reiterates the main complaint of this prayer: "People have certainly heard my sighing, but there has been no one to comfort me." Instead, her enemies have rejoiced over her troubles and over the fact that Yahweh "had done it."

Jerusalem's prayer is that God would "bring the day He had announced so they [her enemies] might become as I am." Several times in Lamentations there is a reference to the Day of the Lord as the "day" of His wrath when Jerusalem fell (Lam. 1:12; 2:1, 21 and 22). But if that day had a *past* it

will also have a *future,* for that is what Zion prays for in 1:
21. Thus all the historical moments when God's wrath was
poured out were but earnests and small tokens of what that
final great day of His wrath would be like.

But what about this prayer that the Lord would do to
Jerusalem's enemies as they had done to her? Must the Christian blush and set aside this teaching in favor of Christ's
word in Matthew 5:44, "Love your enemies"?

Such a strong contrast between the testaments is unfair.
For one thing, the injunction of our Lord in Matthew 5:44
came from the Old Testament (Exod. 23:4-5; Lev. 19:18;
Prov. 25:21-22; cf. Rom. 12:20). Love for one's enemy was
not an optional luxury in either testament.

But there was another matter:

> There are two kinds of enemies. Some who bear ill-will
> towards us personally for private reasons [which] concern
> ourselves alone. When the matter extends no further than
> to our own person, then we should privately commend it to
> God, and pray for those who are ill-disposed towards us . . .
> to do them good, and not return evil for evil, but rather
> overcome evil with good (Rom xii. 17, 21). But if our
> enemies are of that sort, that they bear ill-will toward us,
> not for any private cause, but on account of matters of
> faith; and are also opposed not only to us, but especially
> to God in Heaven . . . ; then indeed we should pray that
> God would convert those who may be converted, but as
> for those who continue ever to rage, stubbornly and ma-
> liciously, against God and His Church, that God would exe-
> cute upon them according to His own sentence, judgment
> and righteousness (Ps cxxxix.19).[12]

NOTES

1. For a fuller discussion see Walter C. Kaiser, Jr., "The Promise Theme and
the Theology of Rest," *Bibliotheca Sacra* 130 (1973), 135-50; Gerhard von
Rad, "There Remains a Rest For the People of God: An Investigation of a
Biblical Conception," *The Problem of the Hexateuch and Other Essays,*
trans. E. W. Trueman Dicken (New York: McGraw-Hill, 1966), pp. 94-102;
Walter C. Kaiser, Jr., *Toward an Old Testament Theology* (Grand Rapids:
Zondervan, 1979), pp. 127-30.

2. C. W. Eduard Nägelsbach, *The Lamentations of Jeremiah,* trans., enlarged, and ed. William H. Hornblower in *Lange's Commentary* (New York: Scribner, Armstrong, 1870), p. 61.

3. Ibid., pp. 61-62.

4. Ibid.

5. Delbert Hillers, *Lamentations: The Anchor Bible* (Garden City, N.Y.: Doubleday, 1972), p. 16.

6. This interpretation of verse 3 renders *min,* "from" not as causal, "on account of," which would necessitate giving *galah* the anomalous rendering of "to migrate (voluntarily)," but rather as "out of" and thus it refers to Judah's troubles *prior to* the captivity. See Hillers, p. 7.

7. The Hebrew expression in verse 7 is *sāhᵃqû ʿal miśᵉbbattehā.* C. F. Keil and F. Delitzsch, *The Prophecies of Jeremiah: Biblical Commentary on the Old Testament,* 25 vols. (Grand Rapids: Eerdmans, 1956), 20:364-65.

8. *pᵉlaʾîm* is related to the noun *pele',* "wonderful" as in Isaiah 9:6, "Wonderful Counselor," or "miracle" in Exodus 15:11, Psalm 77:12, 15.

9. Nägelsbach, p. 49.

10. The first two words, *lô' ʾᵃlêkem,* literally "not to you," have been translated as (1) a particle of *wishing* ("Oh that," "Oh if," "Would that") giving a call for sympathy, (2) a *negative* ("Is it nothing to you?" "Does this not affect you at all?"), (3) a *simple negative* ("This has not happened to you"). Many moderns opt for a simple negative understood as a wish: ("May it never happen to you what has happened to me"); others prefer the negative interrogative.

11. The Hebrew is explicit: *hᵉšibanî ʾāhôr.*

12. Cramer, as cited by Nägelsbach, p. 67.

2

Taking Suffering Personally

One of the reasons Lamentations is so effective in its ministry to those who are suffering is that it deals head-on with the anger of God. Although God's anger is referred to in other chapters (1:12; 3:1, 43, 66; 4:11; 5:22), in Lamentations 2 we find a most detailed and resolute treatment of this difficult matter. In fact, before we have gone ten verses into the chapter there are forty descriptions of God's judgment and anger. Few if any aspects of life eluded His anger.

Therein lies the point of this chapter. Too many would-be do-gooders out of misdirected kindness advise the sufferer: "Don't take it personally!" Or, "Don't think anything about it; after all, that's the way the ball bounces. Things just happen that way. You can't fight city hall." On and on goes such fatalistic thinking.

But all such talk only keeps us from one of the most valuable helps that can be given to the sufferer. Suffering is not due to some blind, brute, dumb forces that happen to come upon me by chance. Rather suffering is an intensely personal experience. And in retributive suffering (suffering for offenses done) it is especially personal since in it I face up to the anger of God. The penalty we will pay for removing God's anger from this kind of suffering will be the loneliness of being hit by a depersonalized grief in which we are objects being bombarded by blind chance and impersonal forces. That kind of world is scary and lonely.

This whole question of divine anger (*ira dei*) has been the subject of some sharp debate in the history of the church. It became known as the question of divine passibility (the quality or aptness in God to feel, suffer, or be angry) or impassibility (the denial of those qualities). Under the strong advocacy of Gnosticism (a philosophy that combined Greek and Oriental ideas with Christian teaching and professed access to truth that was a mystery to outsiders) a doctrine of God emerged that took the strongest exception to any claim that God could feel or suffer anything or that He could be angry.

The second century of the Christian era saw the climax of those Gnostic claims in a man named Marcion. At the base of all his criticism of a God who was passible, one who knew anger and could feel suffering, was his assertion that God must be impassible. Marcion's God never took offense, was never angry, was entirely apathetic, and free from all affections; in fact, He was incapable of being angry.[1] Marcion's agenda is clarified once we realize that he wanted to purge Christianity of every vestige of Judaism. Thus for him the God of the Old Testament was a "Demiurge" (a god subordinate to the supreme God and responsible for the creation of evil) whose involvement in war, suffering, and judgments disqualified Him from being the God of grace and goodness whom Marcion found in most of Paul's epistles in the New Testament.

Thankfully, the church expelled Marcion and anathematized his doctrines in A.D. 144. But the struggle over whether God was capable of having even good emotions and a holy or righteous anger continued in the church. Tertullian, the early church Father, tried to answer Marcion's charges by writing a book entitled *Against Marcion* in which he did us the disfavor of relegating all the objectionable passages of Scripture that Marcion had pointed out to the second person of the Trinity. Tertullian concluded that the Father was indeed "impassible" (as Marcion had argued) but the Son was "irascible" (easily provoked to anger as in the Latin word *ira*, "anger"). But this was almost what later Platonism

did by casting all that was felt to be repulsive onto the backs
of demons.[2]

The church had to wait until the last half of the third century before another writer, Lactantius, wrote his *De Ira Dei*,
"The Anger of God." For him passions or emotions were
not in themselves evil, but avenues of virtue and goodness
when kept under control. Furthermore, God must be moved
to anger when He sees sin and wickedness in men and women
just as He is moved to love them when they please Him.
In Lactantius's own words the argument goes like this:

> He who loves the good, by this very fact hates the evil; and
> he who does not hate the evil, does not love the good; be-
> cause the love of goodness issues directly out of the hatred
> of evil, and the hatred of evil issues directly out of the love
> of goodness. No one can love life without abhoring death;
> and no one can have an appetency for light, without an
> antipathy to darkness.[3]

Of course our problem with anger is that we define it as
Aristotle did, "the desire for retaliation"[4] or a desire to get
even and get revenge for a slight or real harm done to us.
With anger goes the idea of a "brief madness"[5] and "an un-
easiness or discomposure of the mind, upon the receipt of an
injury, with a present purpose of revenge."[6] But Lactantius
defined anger as "a motion of the soul rousing itself to curb
sin."[7] Thus all ideas about revenge, momentary madness,
and the like are accretions and passions gone awry, not true
anger.

The problem is that anger can and does come dangerously
close to evil when it is left unchecked and without control.
That, as a matter of fact, is what is wrong with most defini-
tions of anger; they imply a loss of self-control, an impulsive-
ness, and a temporary derangement. No wonder no one
wants to link God with *that* definition!

On the contrary God's anger is never explosive, unreasonable or unexplainable. It is rather His firm expression of real

displeasure with our wickedness and sin. Even in God it is never a force or a ruling passion; rather, it is always an instrument of His will. And His anger has not, thereby, shut off his compassions to us (Ps. 77:9).

God's anger marks the end of indifference. He cannot and will not remain neutral and impartial in the presence of continued sin. Even though mortals have experienced the benefits of divine patience (which is not to be confused with apathy or complete indifference), the restraint God shows toward us and evil must finally yield to anger when we refuse to mend our ways and deeds. God's delight is in "doing them [and us] good" (Jer. 32:41; cf. 9:24), not in expressing His anger. And even when He must unleash His anger it lasts but for a moment (Ps. 30:5). His love remains (Jer. 31:3; Hos. 2:19) while His anger passes quickly (Isa. 26:20; 54:7-8; 57:16-19). God's love goes on forever with mercy and compassion to thousands (Pss. 100:5; 106:1; 107:1; 118:1-4; 136:1-26).

It is this love that motivates the poet's lament in Lamentations 2. Even though God was exceedingly angry with Judah His anger was not like a hidden force, incalculable and arbitrary, hitting where and when it wished without any rhyme or reason. Instead His anger was measured out and controlled by both His love and justice. It was at once an expression of outrage against the sin, evil, and wickedness perpetrated as well as a personal note of continued caring. Had He not cared or loved so intently He would not have troubled Himself to call His wandering sinners back to His embrace. Therefore, we conclude that suffering is an intensely personal thing. Whether we are suffering because of our own sin or not, we are still highly regarded and loved. No suffering, no matter what kind it is, must ever be conceived as being impersonal and as "one of those things which no one can help." This text urges us: "Take it personally."

THE STANZAS IN LAMENTATIONS 2

Whereas the first lament expressed sorrow over the sad state of the *city,* the second chapter is especially concerned with the *Temple* and the *anger of God.* The most conspicuous subject is the Lord's personal agency in the calamities that fell on the Jews in 587 B.C., but especially on the place of His dwelling, the Temple.

This poem does not divide as neatly as the first one did between the third- and first-person pronoun sections. Neither does there appear to be as much progression in psychological development as there was in Lamentations 1. Nevertheless, we can observe this division of the text: verses 1-10 describe what God did to His Temple and His people (note the forty references to "He has . . ." or "the Lord [did such and such]"); in verses 11-12 the prophet speaks in the first person and describes his own pain and sorrow over this grief observed; in verses 14-19 the prophet rebukes and exhorts Judah in the second person with the first part, verses 14-16, being given over to rebuke and the second half, verses 17-19, marked by stinging exhortations; and in verses 20-22 the nation finally speaks on her own behalf again in prayer as she did at the conclusion of chapter 1.

THE FOCAL POINT OF LAMENTATIONS 2

It is clear that Yahweh, the LORD, is the key subject of this chapter. Forty times in the first ten verses the author makes that point. Therefore, it comes as no surprise that Lamentations 2:17 is the pivotal verse for the whole chapter. That verse states in succinct lines what the rest of the chapter was at pains to point out. The text reads:

> The LORD has done what He had planned
> He has carried out His word
> which He ordained long ago:
> He has broken down and He has not spared;
> He has made the enemy rejoice over you,
> He has exalted the horn of your adversaries.

Jeremiah uses the identical verbs (in reverse order) of the main assertion in this verse in his prophecy against Babylon: "For the LORD has planned and done what He spoke concerning the residents of Babylon" (Jer. 51:12). Zechariah would also expand on this same concept with the same verb (*zāmam,* "to plan, purpose, devise"): "Did not my words and my decrees, which I commanded my servants the prophets overtake [*hiśśîgû,* "to overtake, to flag one down"] your fathers? [That is the precise word Moses had prophesied in Deut. 28:15, 45.] Therefore they repented and said: 'The LORD of hosts has done with us exactly what He had planned (*zāmam*) to do; He has dealt with us according to our lifestyles and our deeds'" (Zech. 1:6). Accordingly, the destruction of the city and its Temple along with the exile of the people could be attributed *ultimately* to the purpose and plan of God even if the people were *immediately* guilty and their sin was the real cause of the calamity.

As far back as the days of Moses the plan of God had made it clear what would happen if the promised people would forsake their Lord and His word. These threatening words were collected principally in Leviticus 26:14-39 and Deuteronomy 28:15-68. Even during the earlier days of Jeremiah's ministry, while there still was time to repent, God had warned them that He would not *spare* them nor would He turn back once the days of longsuffering had ended (Jer. 4:28; note the same verb *zāmam,* "to plan," used in this verse as well).

Thus God is in charge of this world and His is a moral government. What He has ordained (*ṣāwâh,* literally "commanded") shall take place in spite of our little rebellions against His decrees. He can cause our enemies to rejoice over us (cf. Ps. 89:42), and He can exalt their "horn" (an image of power and national or personal strength; cf. 1 Sam. 2:1; Pss. 75:5; 92:10; 148:14). He is a living person and Lord of lords; His word is abiding and true and He is faithful to Himself, His word, and yes, even to His sinful subjects who

will come to realize the hard way that He still loves them
enough to pursue them with suffering. This, in part, is what
makes suffering so intensely personal.

A TEACHING OUTLINE FOR LAMENTATIONS 2

Taking Suffering Personally

Key word: *Reasons* (for taking suffering personally)

1. Because it comes from the Lord (2:1-10)
2. Because it affects God's messenger (2:11-13)
3. Because it provokes such personal responses (2:14-19)
4. Because it makes its complaint to the Lord (2:20-22).

EXPOSITION AND APPLICATION

In a new and more bitterly expressed lamentation the poet
focuses on the helplessness of Zion, the former dwelling-
place of the Lord. This time the poet concentrates on the
inner significance of the calamity as he vividly depicts with
the clear marks of an eyewitness what happened. Since Yahweh is the one who has sent this judgment He is the only one
who can comfort and aid Zion in her bleakest moment. The
dirge concludes with Zion pouring out her distress in prayer
(vv. 20-22) as the poet had urged her to do (vv. 17-19).
Yet, in this the most graphic and most bitter of all the chapters in Lamentations we are taught about *taking suffering
personally.*

1. *Because it comes from the Lord* (2:1-10). The opening statement of the second poem sets the stage for all that
follows; Yahweh has "eclipsed," "clouded over" or "disgraced"[8] the daughter of Zion in His anger (v. 1). The main
point is this: It was the Lord Himself who was, in the final
analysis, the agent of the nation's downfall.

What the first line of verse 1 states in general terms the
next two lines spell out in detail. The tragic theme of the divine disgrace or the eclipse of "the daughter of Zion" (1:6;
cf. Jer. 4:31; 6:2, 23) may be seen in the Lord's casting

down "the splendor (or beauty) of Israel" and in His taking no thought for His "footstool."

Both of these terms are filled with theological significance. "The splendor of Israel" was her Temple (Isa. 64:11; see also 60:7; 63:15) and her "ark of the covenant" (Ps. 78: 60-61; cf. 1 Sam. 4:21-22). Likewise, God's "footstool" was identified in 1 Chronicles 28:2 with the ark.[9] David said there: "I had in mine heart to build a house of rest for the ark of covenant of the LORD; that is[10] for the footstool of our God." The reason the ark was named His footstool is that the Lord was enthroned and seated between the cherubim (1 Sam. 4:4; 2 Sam. 6:2; Pss. 80:1; 99:1, 5; 132:7), which were over the ark of the covenant; thus the Lord's feet rested on the cover of the ark (the mercy seat) and He spoke "from above the mercy seat" (Exod. 25:22; Num. 7:89). So great then was the wrath and anger of God at the depth of Judah's sin that He even abandoned His footstool in the day of His anger.

Verses 2-10 explain what this eclipsing of Israel's former glory included. The Lord is pictured as a mighty warrior casting down:

the buildings (v. 2)
the fortresses (vv. 2, 5)
the kingdom (v. 2)
the rulers (vv. 2, 9)
the strength of Israel (v. 3)
the city (v. 3)
the palaces (v. 5)
the festival (v. 6)
the sabbath (v. 6)
the priest (v. 6)
the altar (v. 7)
the sanctuary (v. 7)
the city wall (v. 8)
the city gates (v. 9)
the instruction of the law (v. 9)
the visions of the prophets (v. 9).

In general, verses 2-5 pictured the destruction of the nation while verses 6-10 tended to concentrate on the collapse of the Temple and public worship.

Three metaphors summarize the national tragedy in verse 3; Yahweh "has cut down all the *horn* of Israel in His fierce anger," He "has withdrawn His *right hand* from them," and He "has *burned* like a *flaming fire* against Jacob." The horn is a familiar symbol of strength and power (1 Sam. 2:1; Pss. 75:5; 92:10; 148:14; Jer. 48:25) and in this context it refers to the removal of every one of Israel's offensive and defensive capabilities including her soldiers, fortresses, and other accouterments of war and defense. Thus Judah would have no power to resist or to take the offensive. Likewise the right hand, usually an instrument of help, had also been withdrawn. Left without power to resist and without the necessary assistance of God, Israel was fully exposed to the anger of God that burned against her as a flaming fire. Verse 4 concludes with the destruction of "the pride of our eyes" (the virgins and young men of 1:18; i.e., the children in whom the eyes of the parents took great delight) and "the tent of the daughter of Zion" (where the daughter of Zion lives).

Gone then was Israel, her palaces, and her fortresses (v. 5). She was left only with "sorrow and sadness" or as in another attempt to reproduce the similar sounds of these two words (paronomasia) "moaning and mourning."

Verses 6-10 describe the destruction of the Temple and all public worship of God. The Temple of God had become a hut or booth,[11] easily disassembled as were the booths made of branches for the great annual festivals in Israel. Along with the destruction of the Temple came the cessation of festival, sabbath, king, and priest (all singulars to stress their unrestricted generality). Many are puzzled by the inclusion of king with priest as if his office also included some sacerdotal or ritual features, but there was an intimate connection between the Davidic monarchy and the house of God. Nowhere is this connection more closely observed than in the promise God gave to David through Nathan the prophet in 2 Samuel 7:12-19. Keil expressed it most fairly when he said:

> This promise, in virtue of which Solomon built the temple as a dwelling for the name of Jahveh, connected the building of the temple so closely with the kingdom of David, that this continued existence of the temple might be taken as a pledge of the continuance of David's house; while the destruction of the temple . . . might . . . serve as a sign of the rejection of the Davidic monarchy. Viewing the matter in this light, Jeremiah laments that, with the destruction of the temple and the abolition of the public festivals, Jahveh has rejected king and priest, i.e. the royal family of David as well as the Levitical priesthood.[12]

The poet returns to the theme of the destruction of the kingdom in verses 8-9. Four weeks after the capture of the city Nebuchadnezzar had destroyed not only the Temple, but also the houses, palace, and city walls as we are told in Jeremiah 52:13-14 and 2 Kings 25:9-10. It happened as the Lord had planned (Lam. 2:8) with the same precision that one would build a city (note that Yahweh stretches a measuring line in order to carry out His preconceived plan of dismantling the city and pulling down the buildings (cf. 2 Kings 21:13; Isa. 34:11; Amos 7:7).

This work of the Lord in verses 1-8 has left the city gates buried under the rubble of this divine demolition and the bars used to brace those gates shut were left broken and useless. Thus in verses 9-10 we are given a quick review of the results this work has brought. Even more tragically the divinely-appointed instruction ("law") on the administration of the nation and the prophetic words and visions from God on Judah's deliverance from her present distress both ceased (v. 9). This is not to say that *all* prophecy ceased after the 587 B.C. fall, for God did answer Jeremiah's question ten days after he asked it (Jer. 42:4-7) and Ezekiel and Daniel also prophesied while the people spent seventy years in captivity. Gone also was the counsel and advice of the elders and the joyful song and dance of Jerusalem's virgins (v. 10), the two opposite limits of the population being used to indicate the plight of all the people, both young and old (a merism).

We may make this long list of the forty acts of the Lord into a principle by noting that this is what gave suffering its personal dimension: it was *because it came from the Lord.* It included:

A triple eclipse of former glory (v. 1)
A divine destruction of the nation of promise (vv. 2-5)
A divine cessation of public worship (v. 6)
A divine destruction of the Temple (v. 7)
A divine plan for demolishing the city (vv. 8-9*b*)
A quadruple effect of the present grief (vv. 9*c*-10).

2. *Because it affects God's messenger* (2:11-13). The personal aspect of suffering can be seen in:

The heart rending misery it produced in him (v. 11)
The hopeless conditions it left all around him (v. 12)
The helpless feeling it left in him (v. 13).

No one had labored longer and harder to reverse the destruction-bound forces within the Judean society than God's messenger, Jeremiah. But now that the worst had happened he did not abandon his calloused audience with a weary wave of the hand and a flippant rebuff: "Well, I told you it would happen." God's love and personal regard for this people can be seen in His sending Jeremiah to express his grief at the hurt that came upon his fellow citizens, nation, and Temple.

"Weep with those who weep"; and weep he did. He mourned until he was worn out and exhausted from weeping. The pain he genuinely felt had enraged his bowels and liver (the organ which in that culture was felt to be the center of intense emotion; in this context, of pain).

The very acme of this awful holocaust came when Jere-

miah recalled children fainting in the streets with hunger and
nursing babies breathing their last gasp at their mothers'
empty breasts while vainly trying to get some nourishment
(vv. 11-12). Against such grotesque tragedies Jeremiah felt
helpless to do anything except mourn and share the load of
grief. His prophetic role as a bold announcer of the declara-
tions and judgments of God did not excuse him from the ministry of giving a personal dimension to the suffering.

He took up part of the awful weight of the pain and expressed his own horror, helplessness, and cry for someone to
heal this hideous holocaust. What was there to say? What
favorable word could he, even as a prophet, put in for the
people? What analogies could be made which would show
that others had perhaps experienced the same thing as the
Jews and had survived to say it did not hurt as much as it
once did (v. 13)? Alas, it was all useless! Explanations at
a time like this were beside the point. The pain Zion had
felt was beyond measuring; indeed it appeared incurable.
Who, asked the prophet rhetorically, could cure it? Certainly the answer was "No man can cure us."

3. *Because it provokes such personal responses* (2:14-19).
Some of the false and empty sources of possible healing are
now explored in the first half of this section (vv. 14-16),
which is filled with the pronouns "you" and "your." The
second half (vv. 17-19) will command the people of Judah
to pour out their hearts to the Lord Himself. We might
organize the abiding theology of this section around the following responses:

> Why did we ever trust such false prophets? (v. 14)
> How will we ever endure the malicious joy of our enemies?
>   (vv. 15-16)
> Did not our Lord warn us long ago of this impending trag-
>   edy? (v. 17)
> Will our sorrow ever find any limits as we cry out to the
>   Lord? (vv. 18-19).

False prophets like Hananiah (Jer. 28) had spewed out mere claptrap (literally, "emptiness and whitewash"). The more extended development of this "whitewash" figure of speech may be seen in the false prophets in Ezekiel 13:10-16 (cf. also Ezek. 22:28).

Others, like Calvin, render these two words in verse 14 as "empty and tasteless or saltless." These worthless prophets told the people what they wanted to hear rather than exposing their sin and guilt. Only by boldly reproving Israel for her sin would they have "warded off the captivity" (a typical Jeremian phrase, e.g., Jer. 32:44). Is it any wonder Calvin prayed in this context?

> Grant, Almighty God, that though thou chastisest us as we deserve, we may yet never have the light of truth extinguished amongst us, but may ever see, even in darkness, at least some sparks, which may enable us to behold thy paternal goodness and mercy, so that we may be especially humbled under Thy mighty hand, and that being really prostrate through a deep feeling of repentance, we may raise our hopes to Heaven, and never doubt that Thou wilt at length be reconciled to us when we seek Thee in Thine only-begotten Son. Amen.[13]

On top of all the physical, emotional, and psychological distress the community had to bear came the scorn, enmity, rage, and malicious glee of their conquerors and all who passed by. They "shook their heads" (Pss. 22:7; 109:25; Jer. 18:16) and "hissed" in scorn (1 Kings 9:8; Job 27:23; Jer. 19:8; 49:17; 50:13; Ezek. 27:36; Zeph. 2:15). "Is this," they mockingly sneered, "the city called 'perfect in beauty' and 'the joy of the whole earth'?" Both those expressions had been applied to Zion by the psalmist (Pss. 48:2; 50:2). Unwittingly those heathen mockers were simultaneously confessing that their hatred was directed not only at Jerusalem and the Jews, but also toward God. Jerusalem *was* "the joy of the whole earth" because it was the source and channel of all spiritual blessings to all the nations even as Genesis 12:2-3 had announced in that earliest and most expansive missionary mandate ever given. How tragic for the mockers; in the very words of their snobbery lay their salvation.

At the heart of this chapter is verse 17, which we have already discussed at length. The wonder of the whole matter is that so few took seriously God's ancient threat found primarily in Leviticus 26:14-39 and Deuteronomy 28:15-68. There was, however, one consolation even in this sad event: If God had proved true and faithful to His promise of judgment would He not also be equally as dependable in the reverse side of those judgments; namely, in His words of promise and blessing if God's people would turn back to Him? He, the Lord of His people, is the only One who can help. It is with Him that the citizens of Zion must do business.

And they did turn in prayer to Him! Verse 18 declares that "their heart," the "heart" of "the wall of the daughter of Zion," cried out to the Lord. That the wall of the daughter of Zion is put for all the inhabitants within that wall (personification and synecdoche) is no more peculiar than other passages in the Old and New Testament that take the frontiers for the country they bound, the house for its inhabitants, or the purse for what it contains.[14] As the Psalms urge the congregation to praise God, so here Lamentations urges them to make their complaint known to the Lord. Go ahead and cry—"buckets of tears" as we say or in the conscious exaggeration (hyperbole) of the text "like a stream by day and night." And do not let the flood of your tears dry up from numbness; be sure to get it all out, *but to the Lord*. That will personalize grief. He too is the only one who can do anything to help you.

"Weep aloud all night long," urges Jeremiah, and with uplifted hands of earnest and distraught entreaty (cf. Pss. 28:2; 63:4) "pour out your heart like water before the face

of the Lord" (v. 19). What the prophet had already begun
to do (v. 11) he now urges on the people of God as they join
him in his lament to God. It was time to pray.

4. *Because it makes its complaint to the Lord* (2:20-22).
The prayer the poet had commanded the inhabitants of the
decimated city to make in verses 18-19 is now laid out before the Lord. "Look, O Lord, and see," prays the daughter
of Zion, "to what nation You have done this." The cry is
not one of reproach but a reminder that the incomprehensible
aspect of this whole affair is that the Lord had not done this
to a pagan nation but to the people and nation of promise.
Such an unspeakable tragedy violated not only God's moral
order but also the order of His covenant that He had given
to His people.[15] The implied question is this: When will the
Lord put an end to all this misery? Can God remain seem-
ingly apart and inactive forever? Is it conceivable, possible,
or even right that mothers should eat the children from their
own bodies and the house of God be polluted with no less
than the blood of priests or prophets? The misery was intense, but so were the implications for faith and theology.

Only in the final verse are the human agents of the Lord's
anger brought into the picture. They came as invited guests
(a figure of permitted rather than directed evil, as in the case
of Satan's permission from God to attack Job) would come
to a festival. They encircled the city and became, in that
phrase which now was a stereotype, "terror on every side"
(cf. Ps. 31:13; Jer. 6:25; 20:3,10; 46:5; and 49:29). The
words Judah had derisively used against Jeremiah ("He sees
terror [enemies] all over the place") now formed part of the
people's own confession and prayer. No one had entirely
escaped the effects of God's wrath, for even those who survived the holocaust were deeply affected and would never be
the same for having gone through all of that.

The prayer of the grief-stricken, suffering man or woman
ought to be a plea that the Lord would:

Remember His ancient promises (v. 20*a*)
Behold the depth of our suffering (vv. 20*b*-21)
Bring a swift end to our misery (vv. 20*b*-21)
Remove His anger from us (vv. 21*b*-22)
End His permission for all the human agents of misery (v. 22).

And on this plaintive note the second lament concludes as did the first chapter, with the matter in the lap of God.

NOTES

1. Abraham J. Heschel, *The Prophets* (New York: Harper & Row, 1971), 2:80; also footnote 10.
2. Heschel, 2:81.
3. Lactantius *De Ira Dei*, p. 51.
4. Aristotle *De Anima* 1, p. 1.
5. Horace *Epistolae*, 1: 2:62.
6. John Locke, *An Essay Concerning Human Understanding*, 2:20. I owe these last three citations to Heschel, 2:60, n. 4.
7. Heschel, 2:82.
8. While most understand the verb *yā'īb* as a denominative verb from *'āb*, "cloud" (hence to "cloud over"), this hapax legomenon (word occurring only once in the Hebrew Bible) may be better linked to a root like *w'b* from the noun *tō'ēbah*, "abomination," meaning "to treat with contempt" or even the Arabic *'aba*, "to blame, revile" and thus "to disgrace."
9. Some commentators misunderstand Jeremiah 3:16 and argue that the ark had disappeared already, but that view fails to notice that Jeremiah speaks of this disappearance as a *future* event, not as something that had already happened. The last reference to the ark in the narrative texts appears to be 2 Chronicles 35:3 during the days of Josiah.
10. The "and" here is epexegetical, meaning "that is."
11. Note the unusual spelling *śukko* (with a *sin* instead of a *samek*). Note also Amos 9:11 in which the house of David in its dilapidated condition is likened to a *sukkah*. Nägelsbach, p. 77, notes four instances in which this same interchange of sibilants occurs in the Old Testament.
12. C. F. Keil and F. Delitzsch, *The Prophecies of Jeremiah: Biblical Commentary on the Old Testament*, 25 vols. (Grand Rapids: Eerdmans, 1956), 20:388.
13. John Calvin as cited in C. W. Eduard Nägelsbach, *The Lamentations of Jeremiah*, trans., enlarged, and ed. William H. Hornblower in *Lange's Commentary* (New York: Scribner, Armstrong, 1870), p. 100.
14. Nägelsbach, p. 93; Keil, 2:397 urges us to compare Isaiah 14:31, "Howl, O gate."
15. Keil, 20:399, and Nägelsbach, p. 95.

3

Finding Hope in the Face of Adversity

Lamentations 3 is distinctive, both in form and content, from all the other chapters in the book. It holds the middle position and functions as the culmination and central affirmation of the whole book.

As for *form* the art of the poet comes to its peak performance. Whereas chapters 1, 2, and 4 have twenty-two alphabetically arranged verses, chapter 3 has sixty-six verses arranged in triplets with the three verses of each triplet beginning with the same letter of the alphabet. Each verse is also composed of two lines (distich) usually in *qinah* form so that there are three words or accents in the first line and two in the second line. This ternary (putting things into threes) division is also carried out in the division of the whole poem into three parts (see below).

Chapter 3 is also without parallel in this book in its *content*. Its opening verse is so startling ("I am the man . . .") that we expect something unique right from the start. But who speaks here? Clearly it is an individual "I" (vv. 1-24) changing to "we" (vv. 22, 40-47) and back to "I" again (vv. 48-66). But who is he? C. F. Keil, T. Laetsch, and D. Hillers quote H. Ewald for the answer: "Who is this individual that complains, and thinks, and entreats in this fashion, whose *I* passes unobserved, but quite appropriately, into *we*? O man, it is the very image of thyself! Every one must now speak and think as he does."[1] For some, like Hillers,[2] this means the individual is not a specific historical figure,

75

such as Jeremiah, but is an "everyman." He represents what any man could feel when he goes through such a tragedy, or for that matter any suffering. This typical sufferer represents what any individual anywhere at any time might feel when it seemed that God was against him and his pain and hurt were intense beyond bearing.

At the opposite extreme are those who have linked the man of Lamentations 3 with an *individual*, such as King Jehoiachin.[3] Others like B. Stade, M. Löhr, K. Budde, Rudolph Meek,[4] and T. Laetsch more accurately identified him as the prophet Jeremiah (even if, in the view of most of these men, Jeremiah did not write the book or even compose this poem himself).

A third view of the identity of this individual is that the "I" who speaks in this chapter is a *collective personage*— Zion represented as an individual.[5] The one who speaks has moved beyond any need to distinguish between the individual and the group and is giving expression to what is known in that society as "corporate solidarity." Thus Jeremiah is that individual who suffers in many ways beyond all others; but he is also the representative sufferer for all Israel by virtue of his role as the prophet of the Lord who pled with, prayed for, and preached to his people Israel. This is why this poem finds no trouble in moving from the "I" sections to the "we" verses (vv. 22, 40-47). What is more, the speaker of 3:48-51 can be none other than the prophet Jeremiah since the same terminology is used in Jeremiah 7:16; 11:14; 14:11; and 15:1 of his weeping over his calloused people.

The sudden introduction of "the man" (*haggeber*) in 3:1 as a representative of all Israel accords very well with Hosea's calling Israel "My son" while Matthew refers "My son" in particular to Jesus (Matt. 2:15). In fact, this same alternation within one collective term between the one and the many can be seen in a number of messianic terms that are deliberately chosen by their writers so that they can embrace the whole believing group in Israel and yet can also be telescoped so as to yield up that final representative in a long line of representatives, namely, the Messiah. Consider such terms as "seed," "firstborn," "branch," "Holy one," "anointed one," and the "servant of the Lord." Lamentations 3 is closest in its corporate solidarity or collective aspect to this last title, "servant of the Lord." Because of the prophet's delegated representative role he can pass easily from his own sorrows to those of his nation; his sorrows both represent and summarize all of his nation's sorrows. In this role and in this chapter we come closest to anything that might be called messianic in the book.

Thus, in a way this last view, which we also advocate, is a summary of the strong points of the other two views. Because Jeremiah is both an individual and a representative of the corporate or collective whole, it is hardly necessary merely to draw principles or struggle to apply this text. He has indeed become a sort of "everyman"; that is, *us*. So we will see ourselves and our own problems with suffering. Likewise, we also argue that the individual spoken about here is no one else but the prophet Jeremiah. And because he suffered representatively as God's delegated sufferer he mirrors perfectly, and by divine design, another prophet who would one day also suffer as did the Servant of the Lord in Isaiah 52:13—53:12.

THE STANZAS OF LAMENTATIONS 3

Although most commentators mark the first main break at the end of verse 18 on the basis of subject matter (Jeremiah's description of his trouble), we believe it would be better to observe carefully his use of the first-person singular pronouns (as we have done in the previous two chapters), which extend to verse 24 (verse 22 with the "we" is the only exception). In this manner we are able to connect his first statement of hope with his detailed expression of distress and get a fuller and more balanced picture. Accordingly, after describing his agony of soul and body in verses 1-18 he appeals to God for relief in the next strophe or poetic paragraph (vv. 19-21) and concludes this first section in the last strophe (vv. 22-24) by confessing his faith in the Lord who is his sole consolation and hope.

The middle section of this chapter must be verses 25-39, for they are set off and given boundaries by the use of the first-person singular pronoun in verses 1-24 and the first-person plural pronoun in verses 40-47 (with the first-person singular finishing the chapter in verses 48-66). Its five strophes and five letters of the alphabet (letters *tet* through *mem*) include one more personal confession of hope (vv. 25-30, similar to the conclusion of the first section in vv. 22-24) and pointed instruction in the mercy and faithfulness of God (vv. 31-39).

The final section of this chapter (vv. 40-66) carries us through nine strophes and letters of the alphabet (letters *nun* through *tau*). In the first half (the "we" and "us" section, vv. 40-47) Jeremiah appeals to his people to return to the Lord and leads them in a prayer of confession for their sin and in a lamentation against their enemies. In the second half (vv. 48-66) the poem shifts again to the first-person singular pronoun and the form of the traditional thanksgiving psalm dominates (especially in vv. 52-63). The unusual feature of this second half is that it begins by breaking up a triad, the *pê* triad of vv. 46-48). But it is clear that verse 48 goes with the triad of verses 49-51 on two counts: (1) the switch to the first-person pronoun begins in the last line of the triad of verses 46-48, namely verse 48; (2) The reference to "my eyes" (*'ênî*) is repeated in verses 49 and 51 and actually begins both of those verses in the *'ayin* triad. Nägelsbach asks, "Would the Poet thus intimate that he has passed the culmination-point of his Poem, and therefore the culmination-point of its artistic structure also?"[6] We think the answer is *Yes,* he did so intimate.

The resulting structure of Lamentations 3 is:

1. Verses 1-24 (Based on the use of the first-person singular pronoun)
2. Verses 25-39
3. Verses 40-66 (Based on the use of first-person plural and singular pronouns).

THE FOCAL POINT OF LAMENTATIONS

Like a pool of light in the midst of the thickest darkness, this chapter rises above all others in the hope and consolation it offers. Its central affirmation is found in the triad of verses 22-24.

22 [It is a proof of] the gracious love [*hesed* in plural form]
of the Lord that we are not consumed,
for His compassions [*raham* in plural form] fail not;
23 [they are] new every morning;
great is Thy faithfulness.
24 The Lord is my portion [or inheritance], says my soul;
Therefore, I will hope in Him.

The proof that God still graciously loved His suffering people could be seen in the fact that they were not consumed. At the heart of this triumphant affirmation is that word above all other Old Testament Hebrew words symbolizing God's grace: *hesed*.

In essence, *hesed* is just an Old Testament way of saying that God is gracious and God is love. The fullest development of this most comforting aspect of the character of God can be seen in Exodus 34:6, "The LORD, the LORD, a God compassionate [*rahûm*], gracious [*hannûm*], slow to anger, and great in gracious-love [*hesed*] and truth [*'emet*]." In other words, what the living Word of John 1:14 was, so was the LORD to His suffering people. The words that describe Christ in John 1:14 were taken, in part, from Exodus 34:6,

"And the Word became flesh and dwelt among us . . . full of grace [cf. *hesed*] and truth [cf. *'emet*]."

Hesed[7] appears about 250 times in the Old Testament. It is extremely difficult to get any one or even two English words that completely encompass the whole idea. Based on the nouns that *hesed* is often linked with we may say it includes ideas of *love* or *compassion* (e.g., Ps. 103:4; Zech. 7:9), *grace* (Gen. 19:19; Ps. 109:12), *truth* and *faithfulness* (Exod. 34:6; Ps. 40:11), *goodness* (Ps. 23:6), and *forgiveness* (Num. 14:18; Neh. 9:17; Ps. 86:15-17; Jonah 4:2).

But God's *hesed* is also seen in His acts of deliverance from adverse circumstances as He acted on behalf of Naomi's daughters-in-law (Ruth 1:8) and David as he fled from Absalom (2 Sam. 15:20). God's *hesed* also can be seen in His preservation of David's royal line (Ps. 89:28) and in fact the whole covenant relationship. But one must be careful not to make the covenant primary and *hesed* a product of the covenant; the facts are the other way around. It was God's *hesed*, His gracious love, which produced, maintained, and legitimized the promises contained in the covenant God made with Abraham, Isaac, Jacob, David, and his sons.

Even now in Lamentations 3:22-23 the solid proof that God still cared for His stricken and suffering people was to be found in the "gracious-love" (*hesed*) of the LORD. The startling fact about this announcement is that it is made against one of the bleakest backgrounds in the Old Testament. It would be as if someone had stood up in one of the prison camps of the Third Reich and announced loudly: "Great is God's faithfulness." That might seem ludicrous enough to bring the scornful sneer of every destitute soul confined to those barracks.

But the situation is not without many parallels. Although six million deaths easily exceed all the deaths of 587 B.C., what shall we say about the loss of the messianic office in the exile of the Davidic king Zedekiah? What shall we say about the loss of God's "inheritance," His place of "rest"; namely, the land of Israel? What shall we say about the charred ruins of the former dwelling of the glory of God—ruins which now stood hideously against the skyline as a mute witness to the absence of God from their midst? What shall we say about the passing away of almost every avenue for atonement, reconciliation, and worship of God? For gone were not only the ark of the covenant, the mercy seat, and the Shekinah glory, but gone also were the priests, the altar, the altar of incense, the candlestick, the table of the bread of presence, the festivals, the evening and morning sacrifice, and so much more. Had God totally forsaken His "everlasting" word of promise and could He now give up on ever providing salvation, not only for Israel, but for all the nations of the earth? The Babylonians appeared for the moment to be the grinches who stole Christmas and Easter. Certainly no one could say otherwise, given the present calamity—and of course that everlasting promise to the contrary.

No wonder this phrase, "Great is Thy faithfulness," springs from the page as the greatest word of hope. But it was not sung (as we so often sing the hymn based on this verse) immediately after a body of believers had just experienced another evidence of God's blessing on their lives. On the contrary, this word came when *nothing* looked possible, hopeful, worthwhile, or comforting.

In the face of the direst of adversities, Israel and we are offered hope. It is a word not about answers to the problem of evil; not a word about circumstances or men and movements. It is not a word about systems of political or even theological belief; it is simply a word about our Lord. He is faithful, He is love, He is gracious, He is full of compassion, He is our inheritance.

And therein lies the focal point of the message for this chapter and, because of its position, for the whole book as well. There is plenty of grace in our Lord; all is not lost. That even a kernel of the people of God remains is because of the grace and love of God. These attributes come new each day, for His acts of mercy come from His compassion for us. The compassionate love of God can be seen in His faithfulness. Hope then is not a will-o'-the-wisp, but it is solid confidence and an assured certainty because it resides in the Lord who is our "inheritance." (The same expression occurs in Pss. 16:5; 73:26; 119:57; 142:5; cf. Jer. 10:16; 51:19.)

A TEACHING OUTLINE FOR LAMENTATIONS 3

Finding Hope in the Face of Adversity

Key word: *Grounds* (for hope in adversity)

1. The Lord's love and mercy to us is unending (3:1-24)
2. The Lord's goodness and control of all our lives is re-assuring (3:25-39)
3. The Lord's forgiveness and answers to our prayers are encouraging (3:40-66).

EXPOSITION AND APPLICATION

The individual who suffers in the chapter is Jeremiah as the representative for the whole nation. He is "the man" who was delegated by God to carry in his person all that the nation was also experiencing; their sorrows were his. This helps us to recognize in one large picture how suffering has a unique and particularized history of its own even while it also was intended by the original author to aid "everyman" and help us identify with him. Surely the way this poem passes so easily from the almost forty references to "I" or "my" in verses 1-24 and back again to "we" or "us" in verses 22 and 40-47 is a strong indication that Jeremiah is not speaking merely of himself or only bewailing his personal sufferings. It was on behalf of the nation (and all of us) that he confessed in verse 42: "We have transgressed and we have rebelled." The lament of this chapter then is properly perceived when it is appropriated as the lamentation of every godly individual Israelite and as a lament which many subsequent godly individuals who are non-Israelites may use in similar straits.

Nevertheless, in the midst of all this suffering three times the strong emphasis on *hope* is sounded: "therefore I have hope" (v. 21*b*), "therefore I will hope in Him" (v. 24*b*), and "there may yet be hope" (v. 29*b*). For the first time in an otherwise dreary rehearsal of gloom and despair comes these shafts of light that surround the mountain peak of truth found in the book. Therefore, we have entitled the teaching outline for this chapter *Finding Hope in the Face of Adversity.*

1. *The Lord's love and mercy to us is unending* (3:1-24). It is the first-person singular pronoun, found throughout all twenty-four verses, that forces us to consider these verses as one section. This division of the chapter has the further advantage of joining the cheerless and unrelieved misery of verses 1-18 with the relief that comes in prayer and in the fact that God's love and mercy have not been jettisoned or temporarily suspended: "They are new every morning; great is [His] faithfulness!"

The opening three verses are thematic in character. The triple prominence (at the beginning of each distich or verse) given to the first-person pronoun calls special attention to the speaker and his plight and thereby establishes the central person of this lament—the prophet himself. He can with good justification claim that he had felt the greatest suffering of all. Further, as a spiritual leader in Judah he was the representative of all who were punished in the same way. Thus he represented a class of sufferers.

The depth of Jeremiah's suffering is set off in three bold complaints in verses 1-3. He had "seen" affliction because of:

> the Lord's "rod of anger" (v. 1)
> the Lord's "lead[ing]" him "into darkness" (v. 2)
> the Lord's "turn[ing] His hand against [him]" (v. 3).

Just as the Assyrians were called "the rod of [His] anger" in Isaiah 10:5, God's punishment is so labeled here and in 2 Samuel 7:14; Job 9:34; 21:9; Psalm 89:32, and Proverbs 22:8. The shepherd's rod (in pastoral and political realms) could be a symbol of the exercise of force and so it was here.

God also "led" this sufferer "into darkness"—a figure of adversity (cf. Job 12:25; Amos 5:18). Jeremiah is referring in part, no doubt, to his loss of freedom and the imprisonment that followed. Likewise, the turned hand of God was His hostile action against His prophet. Even though the verbal idea in this third complaint is future it represents a recurring action from the past and is best rendered as a present tense of a repeating concept, for he felt the blow of adversity over and over again—all day long and continuing up to the present.

The proof of this triple complaint is now offered in verses 4-18. In the first of a series of figures he pictures the ebbing and wasting away of his very life. It had given him physical pain and debilitating weakness, for verse 4 refers metaphorically to his skin wasting away and his bones being broken.

The figure then switches in verse 5 to pressures that came from the outside. The prophet, as the representative sufferer, felt himself surrounded and besieged with bitterness (or literally "poison") and distress. It was as if trouble and calamity were high walls obstructing everything, even life itself.

Another obstruction is added in verse 6: darkness. This verse is a word-for-word reproduction of Psalm 143:4c. So deep was his agony of soul and body that he felt as hopeless as those who had died long ago and are now in the grip not only of the grave but even more tragically in the grip of hell (cf. the word for "darkness," *mahᵃšakkîm*; here and in Psalm 88:6 it is attributed to the "pit," *bôr*).

The final and climactic obstruction and an evaluation of all these feelings of confinement are given in verses 7-9. The Assyrians had popularized a form of torture apparently used as a figure of his distress in verse 7. Prisoners were walled up in extremely confined spaces so that they died very quickly. (The words of verse 7*a* are the same ones found in Psalm 88:8*c*.) The prophet also felt as if he had bronze fetters adding to his confinement. In fact, Jeremiah felt so hemmed in that even his prayers (v. 8) did not appear to ascend to God.

It was as if God had blocked up his way (the sufferer now pictured as a traveler) with hewn stones and had forced him into taking crooked paths and circuitous backroads with their increased exposure to attack from wild beasts and robbers (v. 9).

The figure of speech changes once again in verse 10 and God is depicted as a bear or a lion in ambush (cf. Hos. 13:8; Amos 5:19). But, there is a mixing of the figure here, for the prophet also likened Israel's enemies to lions (Jer. 5:6; 6:7; 49:19; 50:44). Therefore, God had allowed the nation to be attacked and mangled by its enemy.

In yet another new figure in verse 12 the Lord is pictured as an archer shooting with deadly accuracy at his prey. The verse appears to imitate Job 16:12 in which Job also felt that God had made him His target. So intense was the suffering that he felt he had been shot in the heart (v. 13) and made the butt of all the ridicule, mockery, and scoffing of all who looked on (v. 14; cf. Jer. 20:7). Not only is Jeremiah the laughingstock of his own people but now Jerusalem had also become the laughingstock of the whole ancient Near East (v. 14).

Such cruel laughter only added to his grief and the result was like being filled after eating—only in this instance the meal consisted of bitter herbs and gall (v. 15). It was also like eating gravel or stones, for the people's teeth had been broken. The people had been feeding on the stones of Baal worship instead of the bread of the Word of God (v. 16). Accordingly, it was appropriate that they should be covered with ashes (a symbol of mourning) for such a great disgrace as following the cult of Baal and the Canaanite cultic installations. Suffering then for this man included:

Internal and physical impairments (v. 4)
Obstruction of freedom and light (vv. 5-6)
Confinement of movement and prayers (vv. 7-9)
Being attacked and badly wounded by the Lord (vv. 10-13)
Being targeted for cruel laughter (v. 14)
Ending up with deep grief and affliction (vv. 15-16).

The conclusion to this individual lament and the transition to the announcement of hope comes in verses 17-21. We are now told of the sufferer's inner reactions to all that he has been through. Out of the deep gloom of his suffering will now emerge hope. The whole of verses 1-16 could be summed up in verse 18: "I thought, 'My lasting hope[8] in the LORD had perished.'" Gone were (1) the soul's enjoyment of peace (v. 17a), (2) all recollections and anticipations of happiness (v. 17b), and (3) the confidence and hope that the Lord would ever deliver him (v. 18).

This robust outburst of despair, however, is followed immediately by the first sighs that form the basis of his prayer and his hope for the future. The suffering of the previous verses can be measured in verse 19 in emphatic words: "affliction" (a word resuming the theme line of 3:1), "oppression" (cf. 1:7), "bitterness" (cf. 3:15), and "gall" (cf. 3:15). But as quickly as he was tempted by the bitter thoughts of verse 18 he recalls something else in verses 20-22: "If I am going to continue to brood over my deep suffering, I am going to be depressed.[9] Instead, this is what I will take stock in (and therefore I will have solid certainty and confidence): '[It is a proof of] the gracious love of the Lord that we are not consumed, for his compassions fail not.'"

The one cause for hope is the gracious acts of love manifested by the Lord. It is His *ḥesed* that rescues the sufferer from the despair and depression that had threatened to bottle him up forever. Just when he came to the breaking point, suddenly, like relief directly from heaven, came this thought —I do have something to which I can fasten my hope. What about all of God's *ḥesed,* compassion, mercy, and faithfulness? None of these has ever come to an end; they arrive brand new every morning (vv. 22-23). The Lord's faithfulness is great! Why can I not teach my suffering body to "hope in Him" since "The Lord is my portion" (v. 24)?

Even the fact that "we are not consumed" (v. 22) is an indication of God's faithfulness. Here the poet speaks on behalf of the people for the first time in this third chapter, but he will resume this manner of speaking in verses 40-47. Calvin summarized it this way: "Were God to take away the promise, all the miserable would inevitably perish; for they can never lay hold on His mercy except through His word. This, then, is the reason why Scripture so often connects these two things together, even God's mercy and His faithfulness in fulfilling His promises."[10]

What a stronghold for the afflicted: God's gracious love, His compassion, and His faithfulness! If ever anyone had experienced a bleak and depressing situation it was this sufferer. And if he found the heart of his case resting in this one hope, then let everyone who has ever experienced grief on a similar or lesser scale anchor his soul in the same assurance: "Great is Thy faithfulness!"

Was this some kind of mental gymnastics in which the mind was placed above and beyond the matters at hand? Should afflicted people deny themselves all expression of tears and lamentation? On the contrary, every line so far in this book has urged us to work through our grief in part by expressing it from *a* to *z.* But now we are led in an affirmation of faith: "The LORD is my portion [share, or inheritance]."

This expression is based on Numbers 18:20 where the LORD said to Aaron when the tribe of Levi was denied an inheritance in the land of Canaan: "I am your portion and your inheritance." The chief possession and delight of Levi was, like that of the sufferer, to be in the LORD. This same expression is also found frequently in the Psalms (16:5*a*; 73:26*c*; 142:5*c*; and especially in 119:57*a* where it is found practically word-for-word). Therefore, we can say with full assurance: "I will hope in Him." This chapter is indeed about hope, but not hope as a wish with a very slight degree of certainty that we will ever obtain or receive anything; this hope carries solid confidence and the highest degree of certainty because it is well-grounded in the God of all grace, mercy, and faithfulness. His love and mercy to us are unending.

2. *The Lord's goodness and control of all our lives is reassuring* (3:25-39). The dominant thought of this section is struck immediately: "The Lord is good." In fact, all three verses of this triad (25-27) begin with the same word, "good" (*ṭôb*). All five triads in this section (vv. 25-27, 28-30, 31-33, 34-36, and 37-39) begin not only with the same letter but with the same or homogeneous words in each line.

The first word of hope is "The Lord is good." Indeed, the Lord is good to "those who trust," that is, who *wait in hope for Him*" (v. 25). The idea of goodness is presented here in three aspects. First, the Lord Himself is good by His very nature and being. Even when He must bring pain and suffering, men and women must place their hope in God's goodness. The second aspect of goodness focuses on the happiness of the person who has learned to wait silently and endure whatever it is that God wishes him to learn or do as a result of his experience of pain (v. 26). The thought is parallel to Psalm 38:15, "But to thee, O LORD, do I wait; it is Thou, O LORD, my God, who will answer" and Isaiah 30:15, "in quietness and confidence shall be your strength."

Third, it is likewise good "to bear the yoke in one's youth" (v. 27). But regarding youth Nägelsbach warns: "But the idea of *youth* is not to be taken in too restricted a sense. By it the Poet would indicate evidently, not youth in opposition to manhood, but the period of still fresh unbroken strength, in opposition to the period of broken and diminished vitality. He would then understand manhood as included in youth."[11] The yoke is the plight of suffering and indicates submission to divine providence. Thus the Lord is good to those who hope in Him and such hope can be expressed by patience in suffering (v. 25), silence in suffering (v. 26), and endurance in suffering (v. 27).

The next two triads and two letters of the alphabet (vv. 28-30, 31-33) develop this concept of the goodness of God as the central focus of our hope. The first triad (vv. 28-30) states how this experience of suffering patiently, silently, and with endurance is to take place, while the second triad (vv. 31-33) gives the reasons sufferers should not despair in the midst of this experience.

The verbs in verses 28-30 can only be translated as cohortatives, "Let him . . ."[12] The three encouragements of these verses exhibit, as Nägelsbach has observed, a certain amount of gradation: "For sitting alone and silent is comparatively easy. To put the mouth in the dust and yet to hope, is more difficult. But the hardest of all, without question, is to present the cheek to the smiter and patiently accept the full measure of disgrace that is come upon us."[13] Even while assuming this patient stance in suffering the point is that we, like this sufferer, must not give up hope that God shall indeed deliver us out of all our troubles.

The reasons for our hope are given in verses 31-33:

> This grief will come to an end (v. 31, "The Lord will not cast off forever")
> The Lord's compassion far outweighs any sorrow He sends (v. 32)
> The Lord does not send affliction willingly (v. 33).

But some might object, "It is all well and good that the Lord does not send any suffering willingly, but what about the evil and distress that come to us from the malice of men and not from God?" It is to this question that the last two triads (vv. 34-36 and 37-39) are addressed. The answer given is this: There is no wrong done on earth that falls outside the control of God. Man has no power and evil has no free rein to do as it pleases apart from the permitting or directing will of God (vv. 37-38).

Verses 34-36 form one long sentence. The infinitives that open each of the three lines must wait for the main verb on which they depend until the last words of verse 36. And those words should be interpreted as a question: "Has not the Lord seen [the three named human injustices]?" The kinds of malice men can heap on our heads are: cruel treatment of war captives and prisoners (v. 34), disregard for basic human rights (v. 35), and malpractice in the halls of justice (v. 36). The abuse of prisoners is a crime God will not condone (Pss. 68:6; 69:33; 107:10-16). Although the term "prisoners" may be extended equally well (according to the meaning of this text) to all mankind who face oppressive forces from a variety of sources, the text does not forget that the war prisoner or jailed criminal is also made in the image of God and therefore must be accorded certain treatment.

Likewise depriving a man of the rights he has as a man and doing so "in the presence of the Most High" (Ps. 113: 5-6) is offensive. God is omniscient and sees everything that is done and said by all men. Therefore the high and mighty of office and the cheats and swindlers in technique had better take note.

The most frequent way in which human rights are run roughshod over is in the injustices of the legal process. Exodus 23:6 warned "You shall not pervert the rights [or justice] due to your poor in his lawsuit" (cf. also Deut. 16:19; 24:17; 27:19; Prov. 17:23; 18:5; Isa. 10:2).

If our misery and pain have come from any of the above-mentioned sources then we must be assured that the Lord in no way approves of it and has indeed seen it (v. 36). The success such evil men have is only temporary and is permitted by God for His own wise purposes (Isa. 45:7; Amos 3:6). The words of verse 37 appear to have Psalm 33:9 in mind: "He spoke and it was done, He commanded and it stood firm." Everything comes from the hand of God (v. 38) whether it be good or evil.

This does *not* mean that we are given here the origin of moral evil or that God is ever said to be the source of what is morally vile or wrong. The context speaks only with regard to the contrast of prosperity with adversity. Thus for the poet in verse 38 the good is physical good and happiness and the evil is physical evil, distress, and misfortune. And even though physical evil comes immediately from the hands of wicked men, as in verses 34-36, yet ultimately it must be permitted by God, and thus it can be assigned directly to Him in that Hebrew way of speaking that does not always bother with the niceties Westerners insist upon—distinguishing between secondary and primary causation.

Thus the section concludes in verse 39 by returning to the theme of verse 22. Man is still alive and is thereby a sign that the gracious-love and mercy of the Lord is unending. So why sigh? If we must sigh, let it be over our sin. It is this thought that prepares us for the final section of this third dirge.

3. *The Lord's forgiveness and answers to our prayers are encouraging* (3:40-66). Suddenly the prophet shifts to the first-person plural "us" and "our." It is this section (vv. 40-47) along with verse 22 that makes it clear that his is a representative role. He will now lead his people in a confession of their sin and will exhort them to return to the Lord.

Clearly, verses 40-42 are an appeal for the people to pray: "Let us lift our hearts and hands to the God of Heaven" (v. 41). It is time to examine their ways and conduct. In former days of plenty and blessing they had no time to turn to the Lord. Now that the worst has happened they had better thoroughly examine and analyze their conduct and former life-style and turn *as far as* (*'ad* "up to," not *'el*, "to" or "toward") the Lord in a total about-face.

The content of the prayer is given in verse 42: "We, yes *we* have transgressed and rebelled; Thou, thou hast not pardoned." The contrast between "we" and "Thou" is emphatic and specific. The reason God had not pardoned was to be found in the people's sins. His justice had to carry out the punishment.

This divine punishment is again described in the corporate prayer of the suffering people as it continued in verses 43-45. God could not answer their cries for help in their sinful condition. So long had sin festered that God's wrath became a cloud and a veil through which no prayer could penetrate (vv. 43-44). But that cloud became God's chariot, or as we would say His "tank," to pursue relentlessly His sinful people with the thunderbolts of His wrath. So He did not spare them (cf. 2:2, 17, 21).

In his prophecy Jeremiah had warned that that would happen: "I will pursue them with sword, famine, and pestilence" (Jer. 29:18; cf. Jer. 15:2-9; 16:5-13). No prayer could assuage God's wrath until the people turned from their sin; not the prayers of the people (Jer. 14:12) nor even the prayers of his prophet (Jer. 7:16; 11:14; 14:11; 15:1). The wrath and anger of God (see our discussion on Lamentations 2) was the righteousness of God reacting against hardened sinners.

The result of God's wrath was contemptuous treatment from the people's enemies. One visualizes nightmares with hundreds of lurid "open mouths" (v. 46; cf. 2:16). What remained was "terror and the pit" (cf. Jer. 48:43), "desolation and destruction" (v. 47).

In the third line of the triad of verses 46-48 the lament shifts just as suddenly and dramatically as it had done in verse 40 back to the first-person singular pronoun (v. 48). The references to "my eyes" in verses 48 and 49 encourage our breaking this triad and placing verse 48 with the lament against the prophet and Israel's enemies. Thus we have moved to the culminating point of the poem and this device of breaking the triad would appear to signal that fact. There is also a beautiful symmetry to this strophe in verses 48-51 in that the first and last lines give a reason for his weeping: "because of the destruction of the daughter of my people" (v. 48*b*) and "because of [what is happening to] all the women of my city" (v. 51*b*).

The awful state of affairs in Jerusalem and Judah brought such a torrent of tears to Jeremiah's eyes that the smarting effect left in his eyes was now transferred to his soul. Without any relief to his tears he who had risked life and limb to prevent such a calamity now wept (not in reproach of God or his people) bitterly for this same people and would continue to do so "until the LORD would look down from heaven and observe [the holocaust that had ensued]" (v. 50).

In verses 52-54 Jeremiah does not speak merely of himself, nor of his experience of being cast into the pit (referred to in Jer. 38:4-6), but of his pain and grief over the wretched condition of his godly countrymen and the affliction they had to endure both from the Babylonians and from their godless fellow-citizens. It is a remarkable fact, but Jeremiah never seeks redress for the personal wrongs he had to bear even though his so-called confessions[14] poured forth freely in his book. Instead, he was occupied with the sad overthrow of the nation and the horrors that overtook his people.

The godly in Judah had enemies "without a reason" (cf. the imitation of the language of Pss. 35:19; 69:4). In that regard this representative sufferer was like the chief substitutionary sufferer (cf. John 15:21). The figures of speech come quickly; his enemies tried to take his life by hurling him into a pit and casting stones at him (v. 53). Indeed the water swirled over his head. But the "pit" (or "dungeon") here is a metaphor for the "grave" or extreme danger (Pss. 28:1; 30:3; 40:2) and the waters symbolize overwhelming misfortune (Ps. 69:2, 15). Jeremiah and all the godly felt they had "had it": "I thought 'I am cut off [from God's help].' "

This sentiment is an echo of another pair of psalms (31: 22; 88:5). None of these statements could have been literally applied to Jeremiah, for (to take only one case) "water over [his] head" would have meant certain death in that pit. Therefore, he pours out his lament on behalf of all the people. The desperateness of their situation has once again been described. Judah and Jeremiah had little hope of survival, for it appeared that they were cut off from the gracious-love of God. Nevertheless, it was to the Lord that they must turn once more.

The last twelve verses of this chapter (vv. 55-66) are a prayer for deliverance. (Therefore we have a chapter ending in prayer, just as chapters 1 and 2.) There are three parts to this prayer:

Thanksgiving to the Lord for His deliverance (vv. 55-58)
A reminder of all that their enemies had done (vv. 59-63)
A request for divine vengeance on their enemies (vv. 64-66).

Out of the blackest night that had engulfed him Jeremiah "called on [the] name [of] the LORD" (v. 55) as "out of the depths of the pit" (so cried the psalmist in 88:6, 13; 130:1). "Do not close your ears to my desperate cry for help," begged Jeremiah. And God heard this request (v. 56).

In a new burst of hope and joy Jeremiah asserts: "You [O LORD] are near whenever I call on Thee; You said: 'Do not be afraid' " (v. 57). What a verse! Here is another great basis for hope in the midst of adversity. The very name of our Lord, *Immanuel,* "God with us," would be stamped over every success or calamity to those who would trust in Him.

This note of thanksgiving and hope continues into the next triad of verses (58-60) as an amplification of verse 56. Already the focus is beginning to shift to his enemies and their assaults, which he had described in verses 52-55 and against which he will request divine vengeance in verses 59-66.

What the members of the suffering community now plead for is someone to take up their cause and to redeem their imperiled lives. The very life of the nation, indeed the kingdom of God, had been threatened by the cruel, marauding masses of Babylonian savages. They had aimed all sorts of schemes, plots, insults, mutterings, and mockery at the people of God and His rule (vv. 60-63). Certainly the LORD, the omniscient One, knew all this was true.

What this righteous sufferer (and all who are godly) wants is divine vengeance (vv. 64-66). With a torrent of righteous invectives against the enemy he begs God to:

> Pay them back in kind (cf. David's words in Ps. 28:4 and Paul's word against Alexander the coppersmith in 2 Tim. 4:14)
>
> Put a veil over their hearts and seal their doom (cf. the blindness brought on by sin in 2 Cor. 3:15 and Deut. 28:28)
>
> Wipe them out from under your heavens, O Lord (cf. Deut. 9:14 for a similar idea).

As it was true in the Psalms of imprecation (cursing) so it was true here: "These so-called imprecations [were] the expression of the longing of an Old Testament saint [as well as of the Apostle Paul in 2 Tim. 4:14] for the vindication of God's righteousness."[15] They were also "utterances of zeal for God and God's kingdom."[16] Moreover, they were "prophetic teachings as to the attitude of God toward sin and impenitent and persistent sinners."[17] Just as David refused to work his own vengeance even when events placed him in an advantageous position over his jealous rival, King Saul, so Jeremiah never once raised his own hand in vengeance for his personal tragedies and adversities. He was totally consumed with grief for God's people, God's city, God's temple, God's anointed, and, in short, God's kingdom.

It was God who had to be vindicated in all of this mess. He remained the only hope to which the godly suffering community clung. He was their portion, the share of the will, to which Jeremiah and all who put their hope in the Lord held.

Was there and does there continue to be any hope for those who face adversity? There is! And He, our LORD, is all our hope and stay. He is loving, He is merciful, and He is faithful. Great is His faithfulness!

NOTES

1. C. F. Keil and F. Delitzsch, *The Prophecies of Jeremiah: Biblical Commentary on the Old Testament*, 25 vols. (Grand Rapids: Eerdmans, 1956), 20:403; Theo. Laetsch, *Bible Commentary: Jeremiah, The Lamentations of Jeremiah* (St. Louis: Concordia, 1965), p. 388; Delbert Hillers, *Lamentations: The Anchor Bible* (Garden City, N.Y.: Doubleday & Co., Inc., 1972), p. 64.
2. Hillers, p. 64.
3. Norman W. Porteous, "Jerusalem-Zion: The Growth of a Symbol," *Verbannung und Heinkehr* (Rudolph Festschrift: Tubingen, 1961), pp. 244-45, as cited by Hillers, p. 63.
4. Theophile J. Meek, *The Book of Lamentations* in *The Interpreter's Bible* (Nashville: Abingdon, 1956), 6:23.
5. Otto Eissfeldt, *Introduction to The Old Testament*, trans. Peter Ackroyd (New York: Harper & Row, 1965), pp. 502-3. Norman K. Gottwald, *Studies in The Book of Lamentations* (London: SCM, 1962), pp. 37-42; Also Bertil Albrektson, *Studies in the Text and Theology of the Book of Lamentations* (Lund, Sweden: CWK, Gleerup, 1963), pp. 126-29.
6. C. W. Eduard Nägelsbach, *The Lamentations of Jeremiah*, trans., enlarged, and ed. William H. Hornblower in *Lange's Commentary* (New York: Scribner, Armstrong, 1870), p. 129.
7. The literature on this word is immense. For the latest study and full bibliography see Katharine D. Sakenfeld, *The Meaning of Hesed in the Hebrew Bible: A New Inquiry* (Missoula, Mo: Scholar's Press, 1978).
8. Taking "My enduring and my hope" as a hendiadys (two words to say one idea). Hillers, p. 55.
9. The view taken of this verse will depend on whether *tizkor* is viewed as a second- or third-person feminine verb. It can only be third person with "my soul" being the subject of both clauses. The second half of the line introduced by *waw* (*wetāšiah*) comes from the verb "to sink down" and expresses the consequence of "my soul" remembering. Hence, "If my soul meditatingly broods over [this suffering] it will become depressed within me." See Keil, 20:413 for the main lines of this argument.
10. Cited by Nägelsbach, p. 115.
11. Nägelsbach, p. 117.
12. Keil, 20:415-6. The apocopated form *yittēn* shows that *yēšēb* and *yiddom* are also cohortatives.
13. Nägelsbach, p. 118.
14. Usually scholars designate six confessions: Jer. 11:18-20; 12:1-4; 15:10-18; 17:14-18; 18:18-23; 20:7-10, 14-18.
15. Chalmers Martin, "Imprecations in the Psalms," in *Classical Evangelical Essays in Old Testament Interpretation,* ed. Walter C. Kaiser, Jr. (Grand Rapids: Baker, 1972), p. 121.
16. Martin, p. 123.
17. Ibid., p. 128.

4

Putting a Name to Pain

"The tone [of Lamentations 4] is more matter-of-fact" exhibiting "a relaxation of the more intense emotion of the earlier poems [with an absence of] the vividness imparted there by the dramatic appearance of various speakers and especially by the personification of Zion."[1] Now that the zenith of emotion and theology has been reached in Lamentations 3:22-24, the intensities of the "front steps" to that focal point may now be eased and a time provided for quietly "mopping up" what remains of the grief process.

Even though a solid resting-place has been found for the afflicted sufferer in the hope that the Lord's gracious-love, mercy, and faithfulness continue during the tragic and lonely moments of grief, it is still necessary to put a name to pain. Thus, "the metaphors [of Lamentations 4] give handles to the suffering so that it can be grasped and handed over to God."[2]

Nothing can be more terrifying than nameless fear, a form of "fearing fear" itself. Those shadows, which remain elusive and ephemeral, float in a jumbled confusion amidst our fears and tend to frighten us as much as the suffering itself. But the naming process is part of the therapy. It helps us to encompass the formless, shapeless mass of adversities and to give it size, shape, identity, and perspective.

The naming process includes more than simple identification. So frequently in Western society we feel that we have exhausted all our responsibility in the learning process when we are able to label some unknown thing. It is almost as if it will now go away and no longer bother us, for we have given it a technical Latin name in place of some common term for its species or genus.

The truth of the matter is that the naming process must penetrate more deeply than that. It must indeed seek to identify, but if it is to be successful in the learning process (and as applied here to the healing of pain) it must also ask concerning *causes*. This need not be a Freudian search for roots and origins—Why should the naming process spend most of its energies chasing the problem of "then" when the patient keeps crying, "But what about 'now'?" The realities of the situation call for an exercise of love *now* and for management of oneself so as to be accountable and responsible *now*.

Nevertheless, some attention must be given to how we got into a situation in the first place if any profit is to come from our mistakes and if any genuine repentance and confession are to take place. Must Judah (and we) simply be sorry that she (and we) were caught in sin (called *attrition* in some theologies—sorrow over being caught in sin and fear only for the punishment)? Surely *contrition* is better and here we must name the sin of which we repent.

Any other way of approaching the sin that causes *some* kinds of suffering would be a glossing over of the issues, but our relief would be temporary and the guilt would be transferred and hidden somewhere else in our personality. Name it then we must if we are ever to recover; name it—to ourselves and to our God.

THE STANZAS OF LAMENTATIONS 4

Once again this chapter is an alphabetic acrostic, with the first line of every two-lined stanza commencing with the next letter of the alphabet. The only difference between the earlier three chapters and this one is that in those chapters the poems had three-lined stanzas, here they have only two lines. (In chapter 5 the stanzas will only be one line without the acrostic format.) By this device the writer clearly indicated that he was beginning to wind down to his conclusion, not only in his more relaxed tone, but also in the format he had chosen.

The chapter may be divided into three parts based mainly on content (and not on the interchange of pronouns as previously). The first twelve verses name the sufferings that the people endured. Whereas Lamentations 1 focused on the city of Jerusalem, Lamentations 2 on the Temple, and Lamentations 3 on the sufferings of the prophet as a representative sufferer, this chapter laments the afflictions that fell on the whole populace of Judah, including all the classes of its citizens.

This first section may be divided into two strophes, 4:1-6 and 7-11, in which Nägelsbach sees a certain parallelism:[3]

4:1-2	The populace: their worth and their pitiable calamity	4:7-9	The princes: their worth and their pitiable calamity
4:3-5	The suffering of little children	4:10	The sad fate of little children
4:6	Closing theological remark	4:11	Closing theological remark

The second section names the causes for this horrible disaster (vv. 12-20). This section may also be divided into two strophes, which describe the two main causes for the disaster that fell on Judah; the sins of her prophets and priests (vv. 12-16), and the empty trust in the help of man (vv. 17-20).

The last section, verses 21-22, ends with an expression of hope and joy. God will execute judgment and vengeance on bystanders like Edom who maliciously enjoyed the devastation of Jerusalem. But this same Lord will also execute His plan and suffering will have an end—even for Zion! Thus the resulting structure of Lamentations 4 is:

1. Verses 1-11
2. Verses 12-20
3. Verses 21-22.

THE FOCAL POINT OF LAMENTATIONS 4

The verse that appears to say it all is verse 13: "[This all happened] because of the sins of her prophets and the iniquities of her priests, who shed the blood of the righteous in her midst."

The verdict that those false prophets and priests had once pronounced over Jeremiah's head (Jer. 26:7-24) had now boomeranged over their own. They had said: "This man deserves the sentence of death, because he has prophesied against this city, as you have heard with your own ears" (Jer. 26:11, RSV).

Jeremiah was delivered from that inflammable situation, in part because some elders cited the precedent of Micah's preaching against the city and Hezekiah's and Judah's repentance (Micah 1:1; 2 Chron. 29:6-11); nevertheless, the false teachers did extradite from Egypt the prophet Uriah, who had preached a similar message, and murdered him (Jer. 26:20-23). But that was only the tip of the iceberg for those blind patriots who put country over principle and the status quo over the need for a heart-felt repentance.

They misled the people in many ways, but the most tragic sin of all was their murderous and cruel repression of the faithful messengers and teachers that God had graciously sent to the people of Judah in order to avert the calamity that ultimately fell on them. In that sense the false prophets were the real culprits. On their hands fell the blood-guiltiness for all the men, women, and little children who died from the sword, famine, and violence of those days. In the end it was they (not the true prophets who predicted calamity against an unrepentant Jerusalem) "who prophesied against this city" (Jer. 26:11). They had predicted peace, safety, security, and prosperity. Alas, it had not come. Therefore, they deserved not only the sentence of death but also the awful responsibility for every single tragedy that befell the people. How important it is to proclaim faithfully God's Word! What an awful carnage and waste of lives results from the failure of the clear proclamation of the Word, even though it may not be altogether to our personal liking in its call for repentance, coupled with an unpopular prospect of national disaster!

A TEACHING OUTLINE FOR LAMENTATIONS 4
Putting a Name to Pain

Key word: *Areas* (where pain must be named)

1.	In its costs	4:1-11
2.	In its causes	4:12-20
3.	In its conclusion	4:21-22.

EXPOSITION AND APPLICATION

Jeremiah returns to the third-person description and begins to assume a quieter emotional tone now that his grief has found hope and solid certainty in the Lord who is gracious, loving, merciful, and faithful. Once more he begins this section with the exclamation "How!" as he did in Lamentations 1:1 and 2:1. But now the text is able to repeat once again some of the now-familiar metaphors of suffering while proceeding to name some of the causes for it. No mourner could sustain the level of intensity of grief and lamentation that we have seen in the first three chapters. Thus we may step back and take a slightly more academic approach now that some perspective has begun to dawn on our grief-weary hearts. So let us then *put a name to grief* even as the poet did in Lamentations 4.

1. *In its costs* (4:1-11). So valuable and precious were the people of God, began the poet, that they were "worth their weight in gold" (vv. 1-2). They were God's "firstborn," "my Son," "my royal priests," "my chosen," "my holy nation," "my treasured possession" (Exod. 4:22; 19:5-6). Being part of the people of God was no small privilege. But it carried corresponding responsibilities. Although the Abrahamic-Davidic promise of God was unconditional and without any kind of cancellation, the personal application of any

of those benefits was entirely conditional. God could (and did) maintain His covenant and order that this promise be transmitted from generation to generation. Very few if any of those transmitting generations participated individually in those same blessings simply because they fell into habitual sin and refused to believe God's promise.[4] But Israel was meant to be worth gold. Three terms are used for "gold" in verses 1-2: a general term (*zahab*), "finest gold" *ketem tob*), and "pure gold" (*paz*).

That was then, but what about now? They were worthless now—treated like cracked pots. Broken pottery is the ubiquitous feature of every tell (artificial mound from the accumulated trash of ancient cities) excavated from the ancient ruins of the Near East. Tossed aside and left like broken potsherds to litter the landscape; what a waste for those who had been worth their weight in gold. Name the shame and name the costs of their sin.

If verses 1-2 named the costs in *theological* terms, then verses 3-5 name the costs in *physical* terms. So monstrous was the suffering that even though the jackals[5] could draw out the breast and offer it to their young, the people of God were unable to feed their children because of the effects of the siege and famine.

God's people became heartless—even to the cry of babes. They were like the ostrich that had become proverbial for laying her eggs in the warmer climes, scratching a little dirt over them, and then abandoning them to be hatched by the sun (cf. Job 39:13-18). Thus whereas the stork is called the *avis pia,* "pious bird," the ostrich is called by the Arabs the "impious" or "ungodly bird."

The tongues of infants stuck to the roofs of their mouths while young children asked for bread, but all to no avail (v. 4). Even the adults felt the impact of the famine. Those who were raised "on delicacies" and dressed in scarlet were now deprived of both. Now they had to settle for the dump and ash heap (v. 5). What pathetic scenes, but they had to be named for they too were deeply etched in the memory of the author.

The theological summary for this first strophe in verse 6 is a comparison of Jerusalem's destruction with the (by now) proverbial overthrow of Sodom. R. K. Harrison has stated it best:

> For her far more serious crime of rejecting covenant mer-
> cies, Jerusalem must seemingly endure a proportionately
> greater chastisemment. . . . It is precarious to postulate the
> concept of "degrees of sin," since all wrongdoing is abhor-
> rent to God. . . . There are, nevertheless, degrees of culpa-
> bility, as the penal legislation of the law made clear (cf.
> Am. 3:2; Mt. 5:21ff.; Lk. 12:47f., etc.).[6]

So greater privilege brings greater responsibility along with greater guilt when that privilege is abused. Therefore, Sodom experienced more sudden destruction from God but Jerusalem endured the agonizing torment of hunger and thirst with countless scenes of human grief left indelibly etched on all the survivors' memories. Sodom was spared this heartache.

In verses 7-11 the same story told in verses 1-6 is repeated almost in identical structures except that now it concentrates on the grief that overtook the "princes."[7] In verse 7 those princes were *once* ruddy in body with dark blue ("lapis lazuli" (color) beards (*gizrātām*).[8] But *now* that stately appearance had suddenly changed. Now they were as black as soot from the effects of the famine and their bodies were misshapen and distorted from the ravages of hunger and lack of carc (v. 8). Their skin stuck to their bones like dry tinder wood. A speedy death with the sword was more preferable than this slow death by starving (v. 9a). Women were reduced to boiling their own children in order to stay alive (v. 10). The misery was heart rending. But name each pain we must—even among the quiet sobs.

Once again (as in v. 6) a theological summary appears

at the end of this strophe (v. 11) completing the first section. It was the Lord who had allowed all those miseries to fall on His city and His people. What God had threatened had now taken place. The fire of His wrath had destroyed the city and consumed its inhabitants.

2. *In its causes* (4:12-20). What many had believed was impossible had now happened—Jerusalem had fallen (v. 12). True, this city had been entered by conquerors before. Pharaoh Shishak took the city without fighting as early as 925 B.C. (1 Kings 14). The Philistine and Arab invasion described in 2 Chronicles 21:16-17 and perhaps in Obadiah had left no permanent damage. Joash, King of Israel, took the city without an assault in 2 Kings 14 and 2 Chronicles 25:21-24, whereas Pharaoh Necho in 2 Kings 23:33-35 and 2 Chronicles 33:11 appears to have avoided Jerusalem altogether. But none of those incursions wreaked any of the havoc that the Babylonians did; the city was decimated completely under them. That was what was so unbelievable.

Verse 13 then tells why such an unbelievable event happened. The connection between verses 12 and 13 can be seen when the words "This came to pass"[9] are placed before "on account of the sins of the prophets and the iniquities of the priests." This verse we regard as the focal point and pivotal statement of the whole chapter. Other explanations for the tragic events that had fallen on the people, their city, and their temple were merely circumstantial explanations. The real perpetrators and responsible agents were the religious leaders of the day who had soft-pedaled the proclamation of the whole counsel of God in favor of what the people wanted to hear.

Jeremiah had warned those bleeding hearts time and time again to speak the truth, but they persisted in their "shalom" prophecies. Some of the places where Jeremiah confronted the prophets and priests are Jeremiah 6:13-15; 8:8-12; 23:11-36; 26:7-24; 28:1-17.

The blood of all the righteous who had been slain in Jerusalem now stained their hands. Such religious charlatans were nothing less than murderers. Having seduced the population and lulled them into moral sleepiness and eventual destruction they were left staggering through the burnt-out ruins as if they were drunk on the blood they had shed. Like blind men they went groping along the way searching for help in every place except the right one. But no one could touch them, for like lepers (cf. Lev. 23:45) they too were unclean with the blood of defilement.

The surviving populace, which once applauded the prophet's and priest's soothing words of peace and prosperity, now yelled at them, "Get out of here, get out of here, don't touch us"—murderers! Therefore they were forced to wander abroad among the nations like vagabonds only to be refused permission to settle down there (v. 15).

As in verses 6 and 11 so now in verse 16 the poet summarizes the theology of the strophe by declaring that those prophets and priests had been "scattered" or "divided" from "the face of the LORD."[10] When God sends His favor He causes His face to shine on us, but when we must finally be exposed to anger we have to face up to His countenance. Shame and disgrace will be the false prophet's position, for they will have lost all respect in their quest for popular acceptance at the expense of faithfully declaring all of God's word. The words of Malachi to the priests of the postexilic age could just as well have been written of Jeremiah's prophets and priests (Mal. 2:6-9). They too made the people stumble by their instruction so God made those teachers despised and abased in the eyes of all the people. Teachers and religious leaders cannot live contrary to God's way of life or show partiality in their instruction. Such irresponsible living and teaching will lead to the destruction of a nation and to the demeaning of and low regard for the teaching office by all the people.

A second cause for the great pain and grief that came upon Judah and Jerusalem can be traced in verses 17-20: It was their empty and fruitless trust in the help and deliverance of men. The amazing thing is that this hope for help from a human source came *after* Judah had experienced all the divine judgments in 587 B.C. In spite of all that had happened they were loathe to turn directly to God! Their first resort was to Pharaoh Hophra of Egypt. Perhaps he would still come and defeat the Babylonians. So strong was this wish that the surviving remnant left in Judah and Jerusalem broke their covenant with Nebuchadnezzar and even fled to Egypt (Ezek. 29:16; Jer. 42-44), but it was all to no avail.

So deeply was sin ingrained in their personalities that when Jeremiah directed the survivors who had fled to Egypt to speak to their wives about their idolatrous ways, the men with brazen insolence struck back and said:

> As for the word which you have spoken to us in the name of the Lord, we will not listen to you. But we will . . . burn incense to the queen of heaven and pour out libations to her, as we did, both we and our fathers, . . . for then we had plenty of food, and prospered, and saw no evil. But since we left off burning incense to the queen of heaven . . . we have lacked everything and have been consumed by the sword and by famine. [Jer. 44:16-18, RSV]

What a view of history! Revival under Josiah and preacher-talk from Jeremiah, in their view, had brought nothing but trouble. They said in effect: "If we are ever going to experience economic growth and good times again, we must return to our idolatry. Our wives are already doing so here in Egypt; we approve of it and we intend to continue the practice." No wonder that generation was wiped out if this is a sample of the insolence that Jeremiah had to put up with.

Before they fled to Egypt, their lives were hounded at every step by the occupying forces of the enemy (v. 18). Every avenue of escape seemed blocked. Just as their trust in man fell when Egypt failed to come to their rescue (v. 17), so that same trust in man collapsed when they hoped that the

king, the son of David and "the breath of life" to the nation
and kingdom of God, would protect them. But he too was
taken captive, put in chains, blinded after watching his sons
being massacred, and marched off to Babylon to die there
(v. 20). King Zedekiah was not the answer to their problems. Jeremiah had warned them:

> Cursed is the man who trusts in man
> and makes flesh his arm,
> whose heart turns away from the LORD.
> He is like a shrub in the desert,
> and shall not see any good come. [Jer. 17:5-6a, RSV]

This pain must likewise be named. How foolish it is to
trust in men rather than the Lord.

3. *In its conclusion* (4:21-22). This too will pass. The
enemy may triumph for the moment and Edom[11] may jeer
all she wants, but the cup of God's wrath (cf. Jer. 25:15-29;
Hab. 2:15-16) will be served to those nations as well. Thus
the words to Edom (the nation that descended from Esau,
the brother of Jacob or Israel) are ironical: "exalt and rejoice." Yes, have a good time, and laugh all you want to,
but you too will be visited by divine judgment.

Keil, following Ewald, assesses these verses in this manner:

> With this "messianic hope," as Ewald rightly characterizes
> the contents of these verses [21-22], the lamentation re-
> solves itself into joyous faith and hope regarding the future
> of Israel. There is no external sign to mark the transition
> from the depths of lamentation over the hopeless condition
> of Judah, to new and hopeful confidence, just as in the
> Psalms there is frequently a sudden change. . . . But these
> transitions have their origin in the firm conviction that
> Israel has most assuredly been chosen as the nation with
> whom the Lord has made his covenant, which He cannot
> break.[12]

Whereas Edom will yet suffer the disgrace of drunkenness
and nudity, the punishment of Judah's sins will come to an

end. No longer will she go into exile, and her guilt will end because her sin is atoned. Jeremiah had predicted in 50:20, "In those days and in that time, says the Lord, iniquity will be sought in Israel, and there shall be none; and sin in Judah, and none shall be found; for I will pardon those whom I leave as a remnant."

Their sins had been "uncovered" (punished) and forgiven. What a conclusion! 'Tis done, 'tis done, the great transaction is done. Guilt has ended and the suffering is over.

NOTES

1. Delbert Hillers, *Lamentations: The Anchor Bible* (Garden City, N.Y.: Doubleday, 1972), p. 86.
2. Eugene H. Peterson, *Five Smooth Stones for Pastoral Work* (Atlanta: John Knox, 1980), p. 99.
3. C. W. Eduard Nägelsbach, *The Lamentations of Jeremiah*, trans., enlarged, and ed. William H. Hornblower in *Lange's Commentary* (New York: Scribner, Armstrong, 1870), p. 149. The idea is his; the format and wording are largely my own.
4. For a more extended defense of this point, see Walter C. Kaiser, Jr., *Toward an Old Testament Theology* (Grand Rapids: Zondervan, 1979), pp. 92-94; 110-13; 156-57; 233n.
5. Some understood the word, *tannin*, to refer to "sea monsters" (Hebrew *Tannim*), but the word must be regarded as an Aramaic plural with *-in* (Hebrew *-im*) suffix since the verbs "drew out," "give suck" are plural and "their young" (*gûrêhen*) is used of the young of lions, bears, dogs, and similar animals. As argued by William Hornblower in Nägelsbach, p. 153.
6. R. K. Harrison, *Jeremiah and Lamentations* (Downers Grove, Ill.: Inter-Varsity, 1973), pp. 233-34.
7. Not Nazirites but *nezîrîm*, as Joseph who was called a *nāzîr* in Genesis 49:26 and Deuteronomy 33:16, that is, "one who was separated" and presumably an eminent one, or ruler of his people.
8. Hillers, p. 81, reminds us that ancient sculptors represented hair on carved heads by inlaid lapis lazuli and ancient literature used the same metaphor.
9. Nägelsbach, pp. 162-63, following Thenius. Keil appears to agree, 20:437 along with Hillers, p. 82. The preceding verse is complete and v. 13 is a prepositional phrase that cannot stand alone; therefore one must supply a subject and predicate like "this came to pass" or "this happened."
10. On God's "face" used in connection with anger see Psalm 34:16; Leviticus 20:3, 6; 26:17; Jeremiah 44:11.
11. "Dweller in the land of Uz." This may be Job's homeland (cf. Job 1:15, 17), that is Edom. The LXX omits Uz in Lamentations 4:21. (Cf. also Jer. 25:20; Gen. 36:28; 1 Chron. 1:42.)
12. Keil, 20:444.

5

Remembering that God Still Reigns

The absence of the usual prayer (see Lam. 1:20-22; 2:20-22; 3:58-66) at the end of Lamentations 4 is now supplied by the fifth chapter as a whole. It is this final touch that gives unity and completes the book, for when all is said and done we rest our case for relief and healing from suffering when we commit it to God in prayer.

Lamentations 5 is unique in other ways. It has a total of only twenty-two lines whereas chapters 1-3 have stanzas with three lines each and chapter 4 has two-lined stanzas. Thus we are given a signal that things are winding down in a *decrescendo*. Another unique feature is that this is the only chapter that is not an acrostic, even though it imitates the acrostic style in that its twenty-two lines are the same number as the letters of the Hebrew alphabet. Furthermore, the hollow and limping meter of the *qinah* or lament poetry is dropped for the smoother three/three division of the line. In fact the second part of a line in this chapter never consists of more than three words.[1]

So different is this chapter that Nägelsbach concludes "the acrostic is wanting because the contents are in prose."[2] But Hornblower with greater justification argues for a poetical format instead of Nägelsbach's estimate. The evidences Hornblower[3] points to are:

(1) The unfailing mark of Hebrew poetry is Hebrew parallelism. (Hillers[4] found that only three of the total

109

of twenty-two lines did not have any Hebrew parallelism [see our introduction for a definition]).

(2) The prayer is full of rhymes and assonance (words sounding alike).[5] Out of the 134 Hebrew words in this chapter, 65 or just less than one-half end in either -*û* or -*m*.

(3) "In spirit as well as form, this chapter is poetry, and that of the highest order. There is nothing prosaic about it, not even in the recital of hard facts and detailed incidents. As the Song proceeds the lyre is tuned to higher chords than even inspired minstrels often reach, and vers. 14-19, are so exquisitely beautiful that we cannot imagine anything to excel them in all the Songs of Heaven and Earth."

The Stanzas of Lamentations 5

In addition to being exquisite poetry chapter 5 is also a prayer. This is clear not only from the opening word in verses 1 and 21, but also from the headings given to the chapter in the various Greek and Latin manuscript copies of the book, which will often have "A Prayer" or "A Prayer of Jeremiah" or something similar.[6]

That it belongs to a prayer genre akin to such Psalms as 44, 60, 74, 79, 80, 83, and 89 can be seen by noting its constituent parts, according to Claus Westerman.[7] The psalm of "Petition" or "Lament of the People" included the following parts.

1. Address and introductory cry for help
    (References to God's previous acts of deliverance)

2. Lament
    A. The Enemy . . .
    B. We . . .
    C. Thou, Lord . . .

3. Confession of trust

4. Petition
   A. Hear . . .
   B. Save . . .
   C. Punish . . .
   D. Double wish   May God do . . . to our enemies
                         May God . . . to us
5. Vow of praise.

It is clear that Lamentations 5:1 is the introduction and cry for help and that verses 19-22 mark the concluding vow of praise. The material that appears in between (vv. 2-18) has been analyzed in two different ways. The first would divide it into the following sections: vv. 2-7, 8-16, and 17-18. This division, which both Nägelsbach and Keil advocate, has the advantage of ending the first two sections in verse 7 and verse 16 with a confession of sin very much as we saw in 4:6 and 4:11. However, it appears to break another guideline we have been using: the careful observation of changes in person and number in the poem. On this basis it would appear to be more accurate to agree with Hornblower[8] and adopt this division:

Introduction (v. 1)
General description of suffering (vv. 2-10)
Instances of individual suffering (vv. 11-13)
Effect on the feelings of the people (vv. 14-18)
Prayer or vow of praise (vv. 19-22).

It should be noted that the first-person plural pronoun appears almost twenty times in verses 2-10, is dropped altogether in the next section, but reappears in verses 15-22. Thus we are compelled for this reason and for that found in our discussion of genre above to adopt this second approach rather than the first.

THE FOCAL POINT OF LAMENTATIONS 5

Without a doubt verse 19 is the central point around which the circle of the content of this chapter was drawn:

You, O Lord reign (literally "sit" or "remain") forever;
Your throne endures forever and ever.

Calvin's comments are extremely pertinent:

> When we fix our eyes on present things, we must necessarily
> vacillate, as there is nothing permanent in the world; and
> when adversities bring a cloud over our eyes, then faith in
> a manner vanishes, at least we are troubled and stand
> amazed. Now the remedy is, to raise our eyes to God, for
> however confounded things may be in the world, yet He re-
> mains always the same. His truth may indeed be hidden
> from us, yet it remains in Him. In short, were the world to
> change and perish a hundred times, nothing could ever
> affect the immutability [unchangeableness] of God. There
> is, then, no doubt but that the Prophet wished to take
> courage and to raise himself up to a firm hope, when he ex-
> claimed, "Thou, O God, remainest forever.[9]

All else may change, but He changes not. God's throne
and rule over all things is thoroughly opposed to what men
call chance or blind fate. Everything may fluctuate, men
and times may grow harder and more difficult, but God still
remains in charge of the situation.

The psalmist had praised God in similar terms:

> Thy throne, O God, endures forever (Ps. 45:6)

> I have pledged to David my servant:
>   I will establish your seed forever,
>   and build your throne for all generations (Ps. 89:3b-
>   4)

> Your throne is established from of old;
>   You are from everlasting (Ps. 93:2).

Even though the Temple of God had been destroyed and
the kingdom and throne promised to David seemed to be in
shambles, God remained firmly in control; and in no sense
had He abdicated His throne. Thus, through the tears and
heart-rending misery the sufferer is led to the one center of

focus that is available to all who feel the bottom has dropped out and all appears to be lost. This same concept appears in almost identical terms in Psalm 102:12:

> But You, O Lord, are enthroned forever;
> Your name endures to all generations.

We too, like Jeremiah and his people, must not be distracted from coming to God in prayer when we are in similar straits and the agony of adversity. No matter what our sin is, how turbulent the events, or how monstrous the grief we bear, along with our confession of sin there must be this lodestar: "You, O LORD, reign forever; Your throne endures forever and ever." What a solace this is for the believing community in the face of the collapse of thrones, the demise and brutal extinction of one's friends and loved ones, and the awful awareness of human sin.

A TEACHING OUTLINE FOR LAMENTATIONS 5

Remembering that God Still Reigns

Key word: *Obstacles* (to our remembering God's reign)

1. Our condition   5:1-10
2. Our individual suffering   5:11-13
3. Our feelings   5:14-18
4. Our questions   5:19-22.

EXPOSITION AND APPLICATION

In psalms of petition or laments of the people, such as this chapter illustrates, the opening verse usually is an introductory cry for help. It is a request that the Lord would not only call to mind but that He would act speedily and favorably on behalf of His people in light of all that had overtaken them and their subsequent disgrace. Viewed in this way, verse 1 functions as a heading for what follows in verses 2-9 where all that happened to them will be depicted once more for the Lord's consideration and, they hope, His favorable intervention.

1. *Our condition* (5:2-10). Three distresses claim the major attention of the petitioner's prayer: the disinherited condition of the people (vv. 2-3), their lack of the basic necessities of life, and the oppressive manners of their conquerors (vv. 4-10).

The land had been held as a gift from the Lord. It had been promised to Abraham four hundred years before his descendants possessed it. This inheritance was an earnest, a kind of down payment, on the future reign of God that would include the restoration of His chosen people, Israel, to that land.[10] Not that God was partial and chauvinistic in His espousal of the Jewish nation, but they stood as a tithe, a small sampler of the fact that God owned *all* the nations of the earth and that His spiritual reign that had already begun in the hearts of men would likewise have a physical and earthly manifestation. He would be Lord over all in actuality, as He was now in principle and by right of His work in creation and redemption.

Alas, even the houses (v. 2) had been disposed of as the Babylonians did what they pleased. Jeremiah 52:13 and 2 Kings 25:9 expressly say that all the houses of Jerusalem were destroyed. The result was that the whole population had become defenseless (v. 3). There is an expressed simile ("*like* widows") in the second half of verse 3, therefore we understand that "orphans" and "widows" are used here in a figurative and not a literal sense. The inhabitants were without land or property and without protection—like penniless paupers, widows, and orphans.

God's people were "without rest" (v. 5). This concept of *rest,* with its physical and spiritual aspects (see Heb. 3:16—4:11 and the bibliography in footnote 10), is closely tied to the "inheritance" of verse 2. The very basic necessities of life, such as water and wood for fires, had to be purchased from the occupying forces of the conquerors (v. 4). No matter where they went, their persecutors were always close behind them driving them on. They were beset with one oppressive measure after another until they found no rest. The irony of Jeremiah's choosing this word is that that is the very thing God had offered in His promise-plan to the people, which they had refused—*rest*.

The reasons Judah had lost her "inheritance" and "rest" are now given in verses 6-7. In the past, and even now in the present, "they had given the hand" (literally), that is, submitted by way of making alliances with such countries as Assyria and Egypt. That favorite policy of many of Israel's and Judah's kings was detested and strongly denounced by God's prophets, for it meant that the nation was saying in effect: "In man we trust" (cf. Jer. 2:18, 36). Such alliances were not only political or for reasons of defense, but also were for economic stability—"to get enough bread" (v. 6). Failing to remember that it was God who gave her her bread, water, wool, flax, oil, and drink, she, like Hosea's wife Gomer, ran after lovers who would give her those same gifts (Hos. 2:5).

It stood to reason then that a confession now had to be forthcoming: *"our* fathers sinned and are no more; and we bear their iniquity" (v. 7). There was no comfort here for those who had quoted the cynical proverb in Jeremiah 31:29 and Ezekiel 18:2, "The fathers have eaten sour grapes and the children's teeth have been set on edge" (see our discussion of the verse in the Introduction). They too must confess in verse 16: "We have sinned!" When the children continue to repeat the sins and mistakes of their fathers, they too are going to reap the same results. The fact is as Jeremiah had said in 3:25, "We have sinned against the LORD from our youth, we and our fathers."[11] In fact, Jeremiah said, "You have done worse than your fathers" (Jer. 16:12).

The list of horrors continues in verses 8-10. Those who were "slaves" (perhaps "puppets" for the will of Babylon) and mere underlings now became brutish, overbearing monsters who pushed the people around at will. This unhappy situation is commented upon in Proverbs 19:10; 30:21-22;

and Ecclesiastes 10:7. No one can escape their imperious hand. Even their bread came "at the peril of [their] lives." But then, Deuteronomy had warned that such would be the case; they should be slaves to their enemies "in hunger and thirst, in nakedness and in dire poverty" (Deut. 28:48, NIV). What scanty harvests they might be able to eke out of the land would be subjected to predatory Bedouins from the desert (v. 9). The result was not enough bread to stave off their hunger. Thus their skin burned like an oven from the heat of their fevers caused by hunger (v. 10). The famine was as furious as the rage of a storm.

Alas! Alas! Under such conditions and obstacles, O Lord, will You not look upon us and remember our condition? Can we in times like these recall that You are still reigning and Your kingdom endures forever and ever?

2. *Our individual suffering* (5:11-13). Another obstacle to recalling God's present reign is the impact that suffering had on individual lives. No one seemed to be exempt; women and virgins were sexually assaulted (v. 11), princes were ignominiously hung on high poles or stakes suspended by their hands (v. 12), and young men and boys were forced into the heavy work of grinding at the millstones like slaves (v. 13).

Everywhere one looked, one could only see cases of tragedy. So awful was the judgment of God that the people brought on themselves by their sin that no one was left unaffected. Even the young children had been afflicted.

The personal, individual aspects of this national tragedy were never forgotten and never far away from one's mind. Behind every national, political, economic, or religious disaster were countless individuals who had felt the brutal sting of grief and pain, disaster and suffering. It was that personal dimension that occupied the thoughts and prayer of Jeremiah as he contemplated the fact that God was still reigning. Yes, He is reigning; but Lord, hear our lament. See these individuals in all strata of society who have been hurt and are now desperate.

3. *Our feelings* (5:14-18). A deep, solemn dread had overtaken the people in the aftermath of the rush of events from 609 to 587 B.C. How could it ever have happened? A new somber mood with heavy threads of depression replaced their former days of song and dance. Every form of joy, merriment, or conviviality was now gone (v. 13).

The city gate, where the elders and judges of Israel and Judah had sat for dispensing justice, advice, or legal transactions (cf. Ruth 4:15; Josh. 20:4) was now empty. Gone also were the songs and music of the young men (v. 14). Jeremiah once again had warned them that such would be the case (Jer. 7:34; 16:9), but no one had listened. Instead, joy had been exchanged for mourning as the new national pastime (v. 15).

The fallen crown of verse 16 is a figurative expression for the loss of the position of honor the nation had held. And she had lost it all because of her sin. As a result of this divestiture of her pride of place among the nations her heart was sickened, her eyes misty and unclear from profuse sorrow. And all that sorrow could be stated very succinctly: Mount Zion was in shambles, a wasteland over which jackals roamed at will (vv. 17-18). She who was "beautiful in her location," "the perfection of all the earth," "the city of David," "the joy of the whole earth," and "the city of the great King," was now a crown fallen from the prince's head (see Pss. 48:2; 50:2; Matt. 5:35).

The commanding symbol of God's presence among His people—Jerusalem—was now an abandoned ruin. The glory of God had left the city as the days grew more wicked and the judgment was momentarily to fall. Ezekiel had traced the stages in that departure. The "glory of God" left the Holy of Holies atop the cherubim and went out to the porch of the Temple (Ezek. 9:3; 10:4). Then it picked up and removed itself to the east gate of the Temple (Ezek. 10:19) only to go on out the east side of the city to the Mount of Olives (Ezek. 11:23). Then the removal of the sheer gravity, the weight (for so the word "glory" implies coming from the verb "to be heavy," *kāḇēḏ*) of the real presence of the Lord was complete. It was removed never more to return permanently until it reappears in the second advent of our Lord (cf. Zech. 14:4) and the glory of the Lord reenters the millennial Temple in Jerusalem (Ezek. 43:4-5). Once more, men and women will be able to say, "The Lord is there" (*Yahweh Shāmmāh,* Ezek. 48:35).

4. *Our questions* (5:19-22). In hymn-like form, verse 19 completes the preparation that began in verse 17 for the prayer that comes in verses 20-22. But there is more in verse 19. It is the answer to every obstacle entertained in this chapter. God's eternal rule and reign is all our hope and stay during the bleak moments of suffering and despair. That one fact comforted the psalmist so many times that we need not marvel at its central position in the teaching of this chapter. For every *why* the psalmist would urge us to sing a thousand times over "Our God reigns" (cf. Pss. 80:1-2; 89:3-4; 103:19).

But two questions haunted the people. They are asked rhetorically in this prayer addressed to their reigning Lord:

Can God continue to forget us forever? (v. 20)
Will He continue to be so exceedingly angry with us that He will reject us forever? (v. 22)

But surely goodness and mercy (Lam. 3:22-24 and Ps. 23:6) had followed Judah all the days of her life—even during this holocaust. God could never forsake His people. He would need to deny Himself in order to do that.

Since that is so then the cry of their prayer and ours is "Restore us to Yourself, O LORD, that we may be restored" (v. 21). The "repentance" or "leading back" spoken of here is not limited to salvation or even to a restoration and leading back to their land once again. It is the revitalizing process by which men and women turn 180 degrees from the objects of their idolatry and self-ambitions to set their life course with an eye single to the Lord. It is begun by godly sorrow for sin (a turning *from*) and it is completed by faith in Yahweh and His written Word (a turning *to*). It may be diagrammed this way:

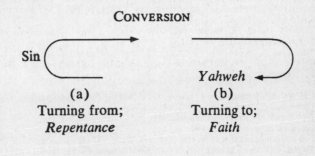

CONVERSION

Sin

Yahweh

(a)
Turning from;
Repentance

(b)
Turning to;
Faith

In this one word could be summarized all the messages of the prophet of the Lord: "turn" (*sûb*). One early message of Jeremiah used this command seven times (Jer. 3:1, 12, 14, 19, 22, 4:1 [twice]). And Zechariah summarized all the prophets who had preceded him and all their messages with this one command, "turn, you all" (Zech. 1:3-4). "Bring us back to yourself and reestablish our relationship one with the other," pled Jeremiah on behalf of the survivors and all who subsequently believed.

The last question Keil understands as being joined to this request for restoration.[12] "Restore us . . . *unless* (*kî'im*) You have totally rejected us." The form of the question, argues Keil, is stated as a possibility to stress that the likelihood of its happening is totally out of the question. Keil thinks the identical phenomenon appears in Jeremiah 14:19.

Of course God can never forget or reject His people, for He has pledged on His life and character that He will perform all that He has promised to do. Thus the book ends on the grand note that our God reigns. He has been and will continue to be faithful, merciful, and full of gracious-love. The Lord, not suffering, grief, or pain, is our portion.

120   *A Biblical Approach to Personal Suffering*

NOTES

1. The apparent exceptions of *lo'* in verses 5 and 12 and *kî* and *nā'* in verse 16 are joined to following words as one accentual unit. Verses 2, 3, and 14 have only two words, but these are long words usually with several accents.

2. C. W. Eduard Nägelsbach, *The Lamentations of Jeremiah*, trans., enlarged, and ed. William H. Hornblower, in *Lange's Commentary on the Holy Scriptures* (New York: Scribner, Armstrong, 1870), p. 177.

3. Cited in Nägelsbach, p. 178.

4. Delbert Hillers, *Lamentations: The Anchor Bible* (Garden City, N.Y.: Doubleday, 1972), p. xxxiv.

5. His count is as follows: *-û* occurs 55 times, 44 as the final letter of words; *-m* occurs 21 times as the final letter; 24 of the half-lines end in *-û;* 17 end in *-nû,* and 9 end in *-m.*

6. Hillers, p. 102.

7. Claus Westermann, *The Praise of God in The Psalms,* trans. Keith R. Crim (Richmond: John Knox, 1965), pp. 52-64.

8. Hornblower, as cited in Nägelsbach, p. 177.

9. Cited by Nägelsbach, p. 194.

10. For a development of this concept, see Walter C. Kaiser, Jr., "The Promise Theme and the Theology of Rest," *Bibliotheca Sacra* 130 (1973): 135-50 and Walter C. Kaiser, Jr., *Toward an Old Testament Theology* (Grand Rapids: Zondervan, 1978), pp. 124-34.

11. Nägelsbach, p. 183, notes that this confession of sin in the midst of a description of their calamities has appeared in 1:5, 8, 9, 14, 18; 2:14; 3:42; 4:6, 12-14; and now 5:7, 16. Note also Jeremiah 16:11; 32:18; and 2 Kings 23:26.

12. C. F. Keil and F. Delitzsch, *The Prophecies of Jeremiah: Biblical Commentary on the Old Testament,* 25 vols. (Grand Rapids: Eerdmans, 1956), 20:454.

Conclusion: Suffering in the Old Testament

"The Old Testament gives us the most comprehensive survey of the problem of suffering from the standpoint of theistic religion which can be found anywhere."[1] Even more amazingly, the Old Testament exceeds our hope for guidance on this subject by indicating that our Lord also suffers along with us, indeed He suffers just as much as we do. His grief comes as a consequence of our sin and our misconduct toward Him. This same principle holds true for a good deal of our own suffering: it arises from improper interaction and a sinful collision of interests between mortals as well as disobedience to God. Because God is so near to His people in the Old Testament He participates in their misery and pain; hence, in ours as well.

But one important point must be made before an improper, unfair, totally destructive conclusion is drawn from our study of suffering in Lamentations. Even though it is clear that this book can point the way in the pastoral task of helping us *cope with grief, take suffering personally, find hope in the face of adversity, put a name to pain,* and *remember that God is still in charge,* it is not the total deposit of biblical truth on this subject. And since it is not the complete summary of all that the Bible has to say on suffering, neither can it be a complete compendium of all the reasons for suffering found in the Bible. In fact, this book concentrates only on one reason for and one kind of suffering: retributive suffering.

On the contrary, there are at least eight basic kinds of suffering in the Old Testament. Each one has a very special part to play in the program of God and in the formation of godliness in each believer. If the little slogan "Be patient with me, God is not finished with me yet" is true in other areas of life, it is all the more applicable in helping to explain the ways of God to men when the problem of suffering emerges.

One of the harshest acts we mortals inflict on one another is the flippant way in which we automatically assume that any pain, anguish, or suffering visited upon another person *must* be as a result of that person's sin. Such unilinear thinking inflicts an unusual amount of cruelty where it is often least deserved, and it only adds to the suffering of the afflicted and their friends. It was just such short-sightedness that finally evoked the judgment of God on Job's well-intentioned but badly-informed friends. Our Lord's sentence of condemnation needs to be etched in bold letters: "My wrath is kindled against you [Eliphaz] and against your friends; for you have not spoken of me what is right, as my servant Job has" (Job 42:7*b*, RSV). Therefore, to guard against any over-zealous erection of a monolithic, one track kind of reductionism based on Lamentations, we feel the reader should be cautioned to put the teaching of this book in its whole canonical context—at least, for the moment, in its whole Old Testament context.

What then are these eight kinds of suffering in the Old Testament? The first and most comprehensive kind is *retributive suffering*. It was given such prominence in the Bible and in Lamentations simply because it is one of the fundamental principles by which God governs the world. Simply stated it is this: If the world is ultimately governed by the one and only God who is righteous and just, then sooner or later in one way or another man's righteousness will be rewarded and his unrighteousness punished. The basic choices of life are good or evil, life or death (Deut. 30:19) when the sufferer has failed to live by the existing norms, whether they be of a ritual, ethical, social, or doctrinal nature.

Often in this kind of suffering the misfortune can be calculated from the very beginning of the indulgence in the sin that eventually must call down the judgment of God. H. Wheeler Robinson summarized retributive suffering by saying:

> This principle, then, is not to be dismissed as one that is superseded by the doctrine of divine grace . . . However harsh may seem the retributive principle when taken alone, and however untrue to our experience of life when the sole principle for the interpretation of suffering, it remains as much part of the moral order of the universe as does the regularity of Nature, on its lower level.[2]

It is necessary to place alongside retributive suffering the complementary principle of *educational* or *disciplinary suffering*. While God must often punish His people for their sins, a corollary emerged in the process of divine revelation; God often afflicted His people for the purpose of teaching them. "My son," urged Solomon in Proverbs 3:11, "do not despise the chastening [*musar*] of the Lord, do not be weary of His reproof." Therefore, the man or woman whom God loved He chastened and corrected often through pain, suffering, and anguish (Prov. 13:24; 15:5).

No portion of God's Word makes this point better than Elihu does in Job 32-37. Relentlessly Elihu applied his case to Job's situation as a divine alternative to the improper suggestion of retributive suffering made by his three hapless predecessors in the argument. It was God, argued Elihu with better insight, who opens our ears to "instruction" (*musar*) by means of adversity (Job 36:10; cf. 33:16; 36:15). Often the sick are "chastened with pain upon [their] bed and with continual strife in [their] bones" (Job 33:19, RSV).

Nevertheless, in spite of all the pain it must be admitted that no one teaches us what we usually would not know better than our God in chastisements (Job 34:31-32; 35:11; 36:22). One whole study has been devoted to this theme alone.[3] Sander's study of the Hebrew verb *yasar*, from which the noun *musar* is derived, shows that approximately one-third of its occurrences (33 out of 92 instances of the word *yasar*) indicate that God is teaching a lesson through hardship inflicted on the nation or individual.[4]

This principle is repeated in the New Testament. Hebrews 12:7 warns that God deals with us as sons when we are chastened even though no one enjoys the lesson while it is being administered. However, when it is over it yields great fruit and peace to those who have been tested.

These two explanations for the problem of suffering lead us to a third. It must be an enigma to many to observe that the Old Testament often portrays the prophet as suffering—especially in his role as the messenger of God. Already we have seen how Jeremiah had such abuse heaped on his head because he delivered God's word without falsehood or adulteration. In Lamentations 3 and in Jeremiah 8:18-21 and 15:15 we have clear evidence of this kind of suffering.

This third kind of suffering is *vicarious suffering*. This principle begins to appear already in the substitutionary nature of the Old Testament sacrifices—especially in the roles given to the two goats on the Day of Atonement in Leviticus 16. All the sin of all the people was ransomed when one goat (in this case involuntarily) gave up his life. The result was that sins were forgiven by a substitute's death and then were forgotten and removed as far as the east is from the west when the second goat (part two of a single sin offering) was led away, figuratively loaded with all the forgiven sins of the people, to be lost forever in the wilderness.

But an even greater example of the vicarious and substitutionary nature of suffering can be seen in the person of the "Suffering Servant" of Isaiah 42-53. The suffering of the Servant is primarily directed toward Israel, even though this Servant is Israel and Judah and comes from that nation. That is part of the mystery of His person; He, like the seed of the woman (Gen. 3:15), is at once part of the corporate solidarity of the whole nation and also the nation's representative and substitute par excellence.

But the Servant suffers not for Himself, but for others. There is not a more passionate demonstration of the vicarious, expiatory, atoning function of the Servant of the Lord than in Isaiah 53. "He was wounded for our transgressions, He was bruised for our iniquities; the punishment that made us whole was upon Him, and by His wounds we are healed" (Isa. 53:5). This formula of one suffering so that others may be forgiven and freed is also found in Isaiah 42:1-4; 49: 4; 50:6; 52:13—53:12. Intimations of God's great atoning act in His Son, our Savior, can already be seen in Genesis 22:12-13 and Exodus 13:13-15.

Contrasted with vicarious suffering is *empathetic suffering*. Grief affects more people than the afflicted; it oftentimes enters fully into the lives and feelings of those whom the sufferer loves or knows. Thus empathy with those who suffer produces a new suffering.

This fourth kind of suffering even affects our God. His feelings of "compassion" and "remorse" are aroused because of the plight or sin of His creatures (Gen. 6:5-6; Exod. 32: 14; Judg. 2:15; 1 Sam. 15:11) so that He "cries out" (Isa. 42:13-14) or "roars" with threatening judgment (Amos 1:2).

The situation is as Isaiah 63:9 describes it: "In all their affliction He was afflicted . . . in His love and pity He redeemed them." At times, the pain and hurt inflicted by erring humans on their God is almost beyond bearing: "Why will you die, O house of Israel? I have no pleasure in the death of any one, says the Lord God; therefore turn and live" (Ezek. 18:31-32). Again in Hosea 11:8 God spreads forth His hands as if He were a distraught parent and asks: "How can I give you up . . . how can I treat you like [the destroyed cities of the plain]? I will not . . . I will not; for I am God . . . , the Holy One in your midst, I will not come to destroy."

Likewise, we are to "weep with those who weep" (Rom.
12:15) and share in others' afflictions as Paul did "out of
much suffering and anguish of the heart and with many tears"
(2 Cor. 2:4). Naomi experienced a similar grief when she
told her daughters-in-law: "No my daughters; it is more bitter for me because of your sakes, for the Lord's hand has
been against me" (Ruth 1:13). The sphere of suffering,
then, is often much larger than those who are immediately
affected.

But beyond "feeling along with others" when they grieve
there is a fifth kind of suffering: *doxological suffering.* Often
God calls His people to go through this experience in order
that His own glory and purpose might be worked out. Here
suffering serves a good end and purpose under the guiding
hand of God.

The primary example of this experience is Joseph in Genesis 45:4, 5, 7 and 50:20. Whereas Joseph's brothers had
intended only evil against their younger brother, God had
allowed his enslavement in order that He might bring about
good and enable many people to live during the forthcoming
seven years of famine. The text of Genesis 50:20 is explicit: "You meant evil against me, but God meant it for
good."

Joseph's suffering during those years of imprisonment had
nothing to do with his own sin, his discipline, or educational
growth; it was allowed solely for the glory of God. The same
situation occurs in John 9 where the man born blind is declared by Jesus to be in such a state not because of his own
or even his parents' sin; rather it was allowed "That the work
of God might be displayed through his life" (John 9:3).

A sixth way the Old Testament treats this subject is to
point to *evidential* or *testimonial suffering.* Clearly the first
two chapters of Job are the classic chapters in defining and
describing this kind of suffering. Although Job would have
dearly loved to know what was going on behind the scenes
in heaven (as the reader does) he obviously does not know.

Job in effect was a test case to show Satan (and would-be mockers of true religion) that mortals do serve God out of pure love for His person and not because of what they can get out of their obedience. Satan's charge had been: "No wonder Job serves You; he is Your fair-haired boy; You have prospered him so much and erected such a wall of protection around him that he would be crazy to give up such a good deal."

Indeed, it was God who had called Satan's attention to Job in the first place (if only Job had *known* that!). God, not Job, ultimately was the one on trial. It must be demonstrated that men and women will serve God whether they are doing well or not. Therefore, God allowed the devil to test Job's allegiance by removing all his possessions (Job 1:9-12) and even his health (Job 2:4-6). And Job still loved God!

Another instance of evidential or testimonial suffering can be found in the prophet Habakkuk's life. When the prophet complained to God about the alarming increase of evil in Judah without any apparent divine judgment, he was informed that God would deal with the problem. Alas, however, the solution was a shocking one; God would bring retribution at the hands of the Babylonians—a feared, pagan national enemy. This led Habakkuk to complain, "[can] the wicked swallow up the man more righteous than himself?" (Hab. 1:13). But there was no answer to the prophet's complaint—at least not immediately. Instead he learned "the just shall live by faith" (Hab. 2:4). Such endurance at once demonstrated the prophet's own innocence and also witnessed to the truth for which he stood. Instead of being some kind of exceptional mortal Habakkuk made it plain that the prospect of Babylonian invasion tore him up inside—from a human standpoint (Hab. 3:16); however, as a man of faith he could confidently assert in the same breath, "Nevertheless, I will rejoice in the LORD, I will rejoice in God my Savior" (Hab. 3:18).

The presence of this strong "nevertheless" reminds us of

another great contrast in that magnificent statement of Psalm 73. The psalmist had almost gone over the brink of despair when he had observed the apparent success and unremitting prosperity of the wicked. Only when he went into God's house and considered the end of the wicked did it come to him: "Nevertheless, I am continually with you; you uphold me by my right hand. You will guide me with your counsel, and afterward you will take me into glory" (Ps. 73:23-24).

In each of those cases a witness, a testimony with strong evidence, was given to the faithfulness of God. Suffering became the tool of our Lord to point to Himself in a way that other kinds of evidences could hardly match.

Suffering can also be used to bring us into a deeper knowledge of our God and the special relationship He has to His men and women. *Revelational suffering* can best be exhibited in the prophets Hosea and Jeremiah.

Hosea's family life was singularly marked by some of the most severe testing any married person must endure. One needs to exercise very little imagination to depict what the tragedy of that prophet's domestic life must have done to him personally—especially as he attempted to carry on a ministry in the very locale of those who knew what had happened to him. The cat-calls, insinuations, and slurs about his wife who now gave her love in prostitution to Baal and to all the idolatrous male worshipers must have often interrupted the prophet's public ministry. But he was more than a match for all such rationalizations and smears. He publicly avowed that he still loved his wife and would take her back home at any time. Furthermore, with a master stroke of pertinency, he pointedly charged that his hecklers were in the very process of committing the same act against God (except they were spiritual adulterers) and God loved them, too. They must repent. No wonder the book of Hosea is known as the book that shows us the heart and holiness of God. If God loves us like Hosea continued to love his unlovely wife, then truly suffering can be revelational.

Likewise, the lengthy story of Jeremiah's physical, spiritual, and mental sufferings is given, in part, so that all the more convincingly he might know and describe by word and life the suffering Judah was causing for her rejected Lord.

The final kind of suffering is *eschatological* or *apocalyptic suffering*. Key portions of the prophetic text expect that God will permit a period of intense suffering just before the end of this historical eon. Just when it has grown the darkest and men have despaired of all hope, then the kingdom of God will emerge in its most glorious moment ever in the universe. The intense days of Israel's suffering will climax in a new exodus under a new Moses with a new David in a new Jerusalem with a new heaven and a new earth.

Some of the major Old Testament prophetic sections dealing with this triumphant moment are Isaiah 24-27; Jeremiah 30-33, Ezekiel 33-48, Daniel 2-12, and Zechariah 12-14. The momentary sufferings of Israel will be exchanged for the joy of new birth religiously, nationally, ecologically, and physically. The Protector of Israel will have arrived on the scene once again to comfort His people in their suffering (Jer. 31:16) and to put an end to the shame and misery of that nation (Ezek. 36:3, 6, 22-23). Out of the furnace of affliction will emerge a purified people (Zech. 13:9; Mal. 3:3) ready for a whole new day.

Suffering then is multiplex in its causes, purposes, and explanations. All attempts to reduce the explanation of suffering both in that day and ours to a single reason, such as retributive suffering, could earn the quick rebuke of God as it did for Job's three friends. Let us be biblically sensitive and spiritually alert to the wholeness of God's revelation, and let us be reticent to postulate total patterns based on the presence of a single swallow.

Let us also bow low before our Maker and recognize His infinite wisdom in His distinctive and numerous reasons for suffering. And when none of these eight explanations, or any additional reasons that may have eluded us here, seems to fit our own moment of crisis, then let us return to the lode-stone and central affirmation of the book of Lamentations: "Great is Thy faithfulness."

NOTES

1. H. Wheeler Robinson, *Suffering: Human and Divine* (New York: Mac-Millan, 1939), p 31.
2. Robinson, p. 36.
3. Jim Alvin Sanders, "Suffering As Divine Discipline in the Old Testament and Post-Biblical Judaism," *Colgate Rochester Divinity School Bulletin* 28 (1955), pp. 1-135.
4. Sanders, p. 42.

Subject Index

Scripture Index

Author Index

Index of Hebrew Words Defined